FROM THE
KING'S COURT
TO
KICKSTARTER

PATRONAGE IN THE MODERN ERA

JULIE AUSTIN

ISBN-0692077308
ISBN-9780692077306

This book is dedicated to my friend and mentor,
TV and radio host Joe Franklin…

who gave many artists their first chance to shine.

Contents

Preface

The earliest known patronage of art in history occurred in the days of the Roman Empire. If we were to cover every year, every country, every continent, and every patron throughout history, this book would never be finished. So, I've had to narrow it down to the time period right before the Renaissance in Europe through to the current times now in America.

All efforts have been made to cover as many areas of the arts as possible from performing arts to visual arts to literary arts, and every type of art patron. This book is meant to be a broad sweeping overview of art patronage throughout history and a look into the future of art patronage. The internet, and other new technological advancements, have added a plethora of ways that artists of all kinds can seek out sponsorship so they can do what they do best… create.

It's never been a more exciting or profitable time to be an artist, as long as artists also learn the business side. Those who do could become the new Michelangelo, Bottecelli, or Leonardo di Vinci of our time.

Introduction to Patronage
Friends with Benefits

THE TERM "FRIENDS with benefits" meant something quite different in the Middle Ages than it does now. The "friend" would have been a patron or sponsor for the artist, and the "benefits" would be room, board, food, and access to bank loans and marriageable women. But the definition of art has remained the same since the beginning of, well, art.

Webster defines art as "something that is created with imagination and skill, that is beautiful, or that expresses important ideas or feelings." For our edification we'll use that definition to include artists of all kinds. Painters, sculptors, writers, actors, public speakers, singers, dancers, musicians, and any other kind of artist who is involved in the creation of art. Art touches us, makes us feel, makes us think, and brings us joy. Art encourages creativity and innovation, expands thinking, and helps us with creative problem solving.

Artists throughout history have used their art as a window into what was going on in society at the time. It has been a reflection of their own and society's attitudes about the world around them. Art throughout history has helped change and improve social issues and built up cultures by forcing us to go deeper in our thinking and push us into action to uplift the human spirit. Just listening to a piece of beautiful music, watching a dance performance, reading a novel, or walking through a museum can give us a greater awareness of the world around us and cause us to reflect on the very meaning of our own lives and the meaning of life itself.

Not all art can be considered beautiful or evoke feelings of joy. Some art evokes feelings of anger, sadness, or even shock and disgust. Sometimes art that would shock and disgust one generation may not have the same effect on another generation or on another culture. Art is a shared community activity that helps us celebrate our common humanity. It connects us to our past and gives us hope for the future. Art unites people through communication. It can be a conversation starter that allows us to learn new things about other cultures and how people around the world actually view the world and how they carry on their own traditions.

Art is something we experience in our hearts and minds that allows us to transcend our daily lives. Keeping art alive benefits everyone. Artists inspire us to be more creative and to see the world from a different perspective. Art has been both supported and looked down on at the same time. We look up to the successful artist like Michael Jackson or Bruce Springsteen but down on the starving artist who is singing for their supper on a street corner. This view is supported by a survey that was done by the Urban Institute. It showed that 96 percent of Americans were "greatly inspired" by and "highly value" art. But only 27 percent think that artists contribute in a good way to society.

When public school budgets are running low on money, it's often the arts programs that are the first to get cut. This has been the case for centuries. Art is almost always on the bottom of the list when money is tight and governments need the money to fund other, more pressing, things. Yet, public art adds value to a city, economically, socially, and culturally. It also helps distinguish one city from another and gives it a unique identity. This takes the creativity and skill of a good artist.

The job of an artist is unlike any other job in the world. Most jobs require a college degree, or at least a resume. But not for an artist. The path to success is much more complicated. The typical nine to five job usually involves a steady paycheck, benefits, and vacation time. But artists tend to go from job to job. Once one gig ends, they're hustling to find the next one. It's like a perpetual job search, and talent isn't always what determines the success of an artist.

So, could anybody be an artist? Sure. But making money as an artist? Now that is a whole different ballgame. The myth of the starving artist has been perpetuated for over 150 years. This is the idea that artists need to suffer for their art to prove themselves worthy, that it should be looked at as more of a calling than a job. The starving artist myth started in nineteenth-century Paris with the Bohemians, artists who lived in poverty but who also lived passionately for their art.

Novelist and poet Henry Murger wrote about the Parisian artists in his novel *Scenes de la Vie de Boheme*. The story was based on his own life as a poor, struggling writer living in an attic. His circle of friends (called "the water drinkers" because they couldn't afford to drink wine) were also poor artists living in the same section of Paris. When Murger's book became a success, the Bohemians became famous. Their story was romanticized, and people everywhere suddenly wanted to live that kind of carefree lifestyle, wearing the Bohemian clothing, and writing poetry all day.

Murger categorized starving artists into three categories. The first were the undiscovered artists who thought that they were just going to be discovered because of their talent without having to pursue it. They were the ones who often died in poverty waiting for their big break. The second kind were the ones who lived the Bohemian lifestyle not because they had to but because they liked the idea of living that kind of 'fly by the seat of your pants' adventurous lifestyle that was so romanticized in the press and in novels and poetry of the era. They could live that way because they knew that anytime they wanted to pack it all in, they had a nice home to go back to. And the third type were the actual working artists. Though they may not have had a lot of money, they had a huge amount of ambition and could live comfortably either way.

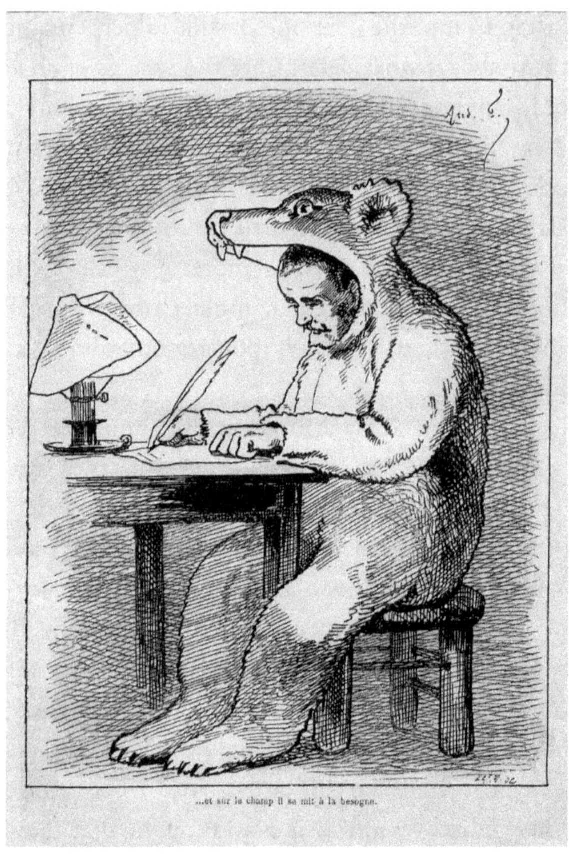

But even Murger himself said that the Bohemian lifestyle should just be a temporary gateway to a life as a professional artist and not a permanent lifestyle. He warned of the consequences if an artist chooses to continue down that path of a life of poverty and ruin and how eventually a choice had to be made. The artists who had patrons avoided this path of destruction, and many of them became quite successful. Those artists were powerful enough to change the culture of that time, like Murger did once he became successful as an artist.

Though *Scenes de la Vie de Boheme* was a success, few of his subsequent novels became as well known. His final years were spent in a country house outside Paris, where he died penniless. Even though the funeral was paid for by the French government, it was still a grand occasion. The publication he once wrote for, *Le Figaro*, publicized the event, which ended up having over 250 luminaries from the worlds of art, theater, and literature in attendance. What I find fascinating is that the monument that was built in his honor was paid for with crowdfunding. Several hundred people donated to the project, and the monument still stands in Paris.

To this day I hear artists talking about not wanting to "sell out" and about how noble it is to give their talent away and live in the moment. The carefree Bohemian lifestyle of the "artiste" sounds great until your electricity is cut off and you get an eviction notice. What they're not thinking about is that the artist always has a master, whether it's an art gallery funding a painter's exhibit, or a production company giving an actor a paycheck, or a record company paying royalties, or even just the public who's buying the art directly. If you're working as an artist to make money, someone is always paying the bills.

The bottom line is that, unless you're independently wealthy and can afford to do your art self-funded or as a hobby, you have to pay bills. And this continues to be a dilemma for artists. Do you continue along the path of the starving artist, doing what you love to do, hoping that one day you'll be rewarded for all of your hard work? Or do you give it up and "get a day job"? Or do you do what many artists have done throughout history, and get patronage?

Patronage, or sponsorship, is financial support from a wealthy donor or donors that allows you to spend all of your time pursuing the type of art you're most passionate about, quite often at your own pace. In Latin the word patron means father or protector. A patron of the arts is someone who protects the arts. That patronage could come from a wealthy art lover, the government, corporations, small businesses, foundations, or the public. The artists are the ones with the talent, but it's the patrons who fork out the money to support them as they create that art. If you do get a patron, or sponsor, you'll be in good company. Some of the most famous and successful artists in history have all had patrons. Michelangelo, di Vinci, Beethoven, Shakespeare, Raphael, and Botticelli all had wealthy patrons supporting them in their careers.

A modern example of one of the most interesting and enduring patronage relationships is between playwright Charles Mee and his friend, philanthropist Richard B. Fisher and his wife Jeanne. It's a good example of how patronage, or sponsorship, isn't just about getting money to create art. It's about a partnership. The partnership of Mee and the Fishers began long before Mee was a well-known playwright or Fisher was a well-known Wall Street tycoon.

Charles Mee decided to take his wife Suzi and their kids on a long summer vacation near the Catskills. So they rented a house in Haines Fall, New York. As fate would have it, Richard Fisher took his wife and kids to their summer home there as well. Richard's wife Emily had put together a recreation program for the families in the community and the Mee children joined in. This is where Charles Mee and Richard Fisher would meet and strike up a lifelong friendship.

They quickly found they had a lot in common, including the fact that they both were stricken with polio as kids and both struggled to overcome it. Over the following years, their friendship would deepen even as Mee's income went down and Fisher's kept climbing. Eventually Mee pulled himself out of debt and achieved some degree of success with his writing. But he still had to hold down a regular job in order to support his wife and kids. He finally decided to write a letter to his old friend Richard Fisher and propose starting a playwriting business together. Mee would supply the writing and Fisher, the money. Instead Fisher proposed something completely different. He wanted to give him enough money to support his wife and kids, while letting him write whatever he wanted without interference.

So there it was. Complete freedom to write whatever he wanted, whenever he wanted, without anyone telling him what to do. It was unheard of, but it was a great artist-patron relationship that would last until Richard passed away and continued with Richard's new wife Jeanne. Theirs was truly a "friends with benefits" arrangement.

How Virginia Sherwood Fletcher Bach Made the Space Patrol Book Possible

By Jean-Noel Bassior, CEO of Speaker Services

Where did you meet your patron?

One day I heard a commotion in the hall outside my apartment. Turns out my neighbor, Virginia Bach, had spotted water leaking from a broken pipe. After management was called, we lingered, talking, and she remarked that I seemed upset about something. I hardly knew her, but found myself confiding that just that morning, I'd lost my savings in the stock market crash (it was the year 2000), and now I'd never be able to take time off to write my book about the dawn of live TV.

Virginia asked about the project, and I told her I'd been collecting interviews for 20 years from pioneers in early television who worked at ABC. As a journalist, I'd written a story for a leading film magazine about Space Patrol, a series that touched me deeply as a child; now I wanted to expand it into a tome about the hair-raising days of early live TV, where anything could go wrong—and often did—before millions of viewers. I had boxes of research and dozens of taped interviews, but my full-time job as a reporter never allowed me enough time to devote to the book. It had grown to a massive project with hundreds of pages of research and demanded a block of time that always seemed just beyond reach.

Virginia asked how much money I'd need to complete the project, and I told her maybe $12,000. That was a wild guess—I wasn't prepared for the question and hadn't really thought it through. Then, to my shock, surprise and delight, she said that wasn't a problem, and she would talk to her broker and withdraw the money from her investment account.

Of course, I could hardly believe what I was hearing, but a few days later, we drove to her broker's office in Beverly Hills and the check was waiting, as promised. I was stunned, and immediately began work on the book.

Over the next few months, as I devoted full time to the project, I realized that I had underestimated the time and money necessary to complete it. But by that time, I had pages to read to Virginia, and we both saw that this was a massive undertaking that was going to go on for a while. And so, another trip to her broker, and another check. Unbelievable.

And so it went, for the next three years. During that time, I continued to work as a journalist, since being freelance, I couldn't drop out of sight and risk losing ties with my editors at major magazines; also, as generous as Virginia's funding was, I wanted to contribute what I could and make her checks last as long as possible. Still, I was able to drastically cut back on my work, take fewer assignments, and devote precious blocks of time to the book, which began to take shape and expand beyond anything I'd imagined.

In the end, Virginia gave me a total of $68,000 dollars, which allowed me to complete a book that turned out better than I ever thought possible. Did she leave me alone during that halcyon time? No. She rode me hard, calling frequently, and needing companionship. Of course, being enormously grateful to her, I wanted to do anything I could, so, to some extent, I was at her beck and call.

But beyond the control she now exercised over my life, there was a sincere desire on her part to see this story told. She and her late husband, famed cartoonist Mickey Bach, had rubbed shoulders with both Hollywood elite and Los Angeles high society in the era I was writing about (1940s-50s). Those years had been the best time of her life, and she truly wanted to preserve this slice of Hollywood history. As I excitedly read her excerpts from the book that was taking shape, we both sensed that this project had an aura of magic that would preserve those days forever.

Did she have a history of sponsoring artists? Own a foundation?

Virginia funded two businesses that I know of, and possibly more. She helped a man create a company so he could market an herbal supplement, because she believed in it. And when she discovered that her part-time caretaker had a great recipe for a soy-meat substitute, she gave the woman enough money to open a vegetarian restaurant.

What was the book about?

My book, Space Patrol: Missions of Daring in the Name of Early Television, *is about the dawn of early, live television in Los Angeles in the late 1940s-early 1950s as seen through the wildly popular TV series,* Space Patrol *(which inspired* Star Trek*). It's a mainstream book (not self-published) and can be found on* Amazon.

Why did she want to sponsor you?

Virginia loved the era I was writing about because she had lived it. She and her late husband, cartoonist Mickey Bach (known for his nationally syndicated "Word a Day" comic strip) had been part of the arts community in Los Angeles, and they socialized with TV and screen actors of the day. Virginia remembered Los Angeles in the exciting post-war years when television was being invented and wanted to preserve that piece of Hollywood history.

How long did it take to write? Is that all you did during that time?

It took three years to write the book, although during that time I continued working as a celebrity journalist and did interviews with Shirley MacLaine, Larry King, and others. However, I was able to cut back on my work, and this gave me the time I needed to focus on the book. I devoted about 2/3 of my time to the book and 1/3 to journalism. Had I not had Virginia's funding, I could not have written the book, as I had to work full-time as a journalist to support myself. Her subsidy made the book possible.

What did it lead to? Any other jobs?

No. Just a lot of good publicity, talk show interviews on main-stream media, and the possibility of making the book into a movie one day, which I'm working on now.

Did the book make money?

Yes. I had a mainstream publisher, so only received 10-12% of the cover price, but it did make a few thousand dollars, and I still continue to receive royalties. These can increase, depending on how much I publicize the book, which is still in print. (The book was later released by my publisher (McFarland) in both paperback and Kindle editions.)

Did she want a ROI or something else in return? Was it a passion project for her?

Virginia acted at first as if the money she gave me was a loan, but as the amount grew, I think she realized that I would not be able to pay her back right away, if ever. She put no pressure on me to make payments—that was left open and vague. I think she knew I probably would not be able to pay her back in her lifetime, as she was in her early 90s. It really was totally a passion project for her, and she passed away a couple of years after the book was published.

Art patronage has been a part of our history since ancient days. We know Roman citizens became patrons, or protectors, of foreigners. The relationship was known as "clientele," where a patron, or protector, took on responsibility for a foreigner. This concept grew during the Medieval and Renaissance eras and turned into the protection and sponsorship of artists by princes and nobles. As time went on, the patron and artist relationship grew more public and started evolving into much more of a trend that continues to this day.

The Romans didn't use the word patron, which means a formal agreement based on reciprocal rights and obligations. They used the word 'amici' or friend and developed relationships with the artists they helped. But the patrons made it clear that they wanted praise in return for their sponsorship. And the artists gave them plenty of it, writing letters that bordered on love letters and dedicating their art to them.[1]

Social class in ancient Rome was based on hierarchy. Having a wealthy patron allowed you to move around in different social networks. Some writers who were already in a higher social class just wanted patrons for extra income. But the writer had to serve some use to the patron besides just having good writing skills. It's the same today. Just being a talented artist doesn't mean much to a sponsor. You also have to bring them a ROI (Return on Investment). Unless you happen to have a patronage relationship like Charles Mee or Jean-Noel Bassior.

In ancient Rome, poets were also public speakers. But public speaking was considered a calling, and therefore it was illegal to make money from it. Augustus put a ban on speakers getting paid money or gifts and this lasted for sixty years. When Claudius came into power he decided to lift the ban. But the public was outraged. They came out in droves to protest. Claudius ended up lowering the amount of money speakers could make and slapped them with harsh penalties if they went over that amount. But poets and speakers had bills to pay and always found other ways around the situation, like getting a patron.

Since they weren't able to take money from their patrons, they would either live in their homes or have their rent paid. They would

---

1 For more on this see, Barbara K. Gold, ed. *Literary and Art Patronage in Ancient Rome*, Austin: University of Texas Press, 1982.

eat their food, be taken to lavish dinners, parties, circuses, and the gladiator games. Some artists would have a single wealthy and powerful patron and they would work exclusively for them. They often rubbed elbows with the patron's influential friends. Access to the high society world was a valuable perk. Many of them got large bank loans on easy terms, legal representation in court, a wife with a large dowry, backroom business deals, and cushy government jobs. In other words, friends with benefits.

The wealthy have been footing the bill for artists for centuries. In ancient Greece, choregoi were wealthy Athenian citizens who financed dramatic productions that were not sponsored by the government. Choregoi were appointed from among the Athenian citizens of great wealth, and as such it was an honor but also a duty. It was designed to improve economic stability by using private monies to fund public good. Choregoi paid for all aspects of production—costumes, rehearsals, chorus expenditures, scenery, props, masks, special effects, and musicians. The playwright and the choregoi both reaped the rewards of a successful win in competitions.

Artists with patrons had the time and money to practice and perfect their skills, while artists without patrons often lived in poverty. Centuries ago, artists without patrons were relegated to being craftsmen and tradesmen. And, like today, the artists without money or patrons often struggled in obscurity. You could have read your work in a public place, but if you didn't have a wealthy patron who paid off crowd members to applaud in the right places you might have been booed off the stage. The patrons also had to make sure there was ample security to ensure your safety. There were also private readings at dinner parties held by the patron and attended by other wealthy and influential people. Promotion and publicity was as important to an author then as it is today.

The majority of authors in the Middle Ages, like the majority of authors today, were not able to make a living from their books alone. They had to do other things like public speaking and teaching. There was no Middle Ages equivalent for Amazon or Barnes and Noble and authors got a lump sum for the publishing of their work, but they didn't get royalties because there was no legal protection. Anyone could copy the book and either sell it or give it away.

Actors during Shakespeare's day were highly respected if they had a patron to help them financially. Actors who didn't usually traveled and lived on the road. They had a much lower status and went from town to town trying to hustle up enough work to survive. But once they were able to attract a patron they no longer had to do that, and their career as an artist was secure.

What starts out as a passion to create, even when you're broke, can easily sap the strongest artist's passion if it goes on for too long. This is evidenced by the sheer number or actors, singers, dancers, and other artists who eventually discover that the price for being an artist is just too high, and waiting tables, tending bar, and driving for Uber or Lyft while waiting for that big break usually takes its toll. The initial excitement they had in the beginning of "making it big" or even making a living as an artist turns to frustration and fatigue.

Too many artists who go into the industry with big hopes and dreams figure out that Murger was right: Trying to go about it the normal, traditional route is daunting. But it doesn't have to be, especially today. Artists are now able to bypass that starving artist route and carve out their own path by raising the financing themselves to create their own projects. Never before have artists of all kinds had so much access to the tools for creating their own careers in the art and entertainment worlds. Or, like Charles Mee and Jean Noel Bassior, they can obtain a wealthy patron to foot the bills while they spend their time on their art—time that's desperately needed to write novels, pen screenplays, make films, and creatively fail a little without worrying that it may be the only chance you'll get as an artist.

For an artist, that freedom is very valuable and takes off a lot of the stress allowing them to do their best work. For Charles Mee, his productivity skyrocketed after getting his unencumbered patronage. He was suddenly cranking out three plays a year. And it wasn't material he was forced to write because he needed to please a client or "sell out" to pay the bills. He worked on only the plays he wanted to write.

Throughout history, patronage has played a vital role in the development and the sustainability of art. Changes in patronage would affect changes in art and in culture itself. The role of the patron has also fluctuated throughout history. Patrons needed artists as much as artists needed them. Patrons benefited from the relationship because of their social status and standing in the community. A patron who sponsored numerous artists was seen as having substantial wealth and a higher ranking in the community. When their protégés became more well-known, the patron's prestige increased. The family image benefitted by donating art to the city or by taking artists under their wing. It brought respect to the patron, but it also made them more humble in the eyes of the community.

Wealthy patrons liked surrounding themselves with artists because they were often entertaining and adventurous. Socializing and courting patrons has always been a time consuming task, even today. Wealthy men in upper class society, much like today, earned passive income, not salaried income. They were expected to have a large entourage to advertise their importance in society, and artists were expected to show up at dinner parties with their patrons. The relationship between artist and patron is unique to each situation. In the Roman Empire, having a patron was a respectable career. It was actually the most popular career for a man of modest means and one that young men would pursue just like they would a career as a teacher or a doctor. Unemployment was very high, and so few jobs were created because many of the respectable professions weren't paid positions.

Writer Samuel Johnson began looking for a patron among the aristocracy and found one in Lord Chesterfield. Or so he thought. Johnson began work on *A Dictionary of the English Language*. It wasn't the first dictionary that had ever been written, but it did have a lasting impact on the English language. Johnson was excited about getting support from Lord Chesterfield, and Chesterfield seemed excited about giving his patronage. He also expected to get credit on the book when it was finished. But after seven years of struggling alone to get the book published, Johnson became frustrated at Chesterfield's half-hearted attempt to help him. Johnson ended up financing it himself. Once Lord Chesterfield realized the dictionary was finished and was becoming a success, Chesterfield then agreed to help him. But at that point it was too late.

Plenty of artists today find themselves in that position. Everyone wants you when you're a star, but nobody wants you when you're struggling. Johnson actually added the word "patron" to the dictionary with this definition: "One who countenances, supports, or protects. Commonly a wretch who supports with insolence, and is paid with flattery." Later a famous letter to Chesterfield began circulating. The letter read:

> *Is not a patron, my Lord, one who looks with unconcern on a man struggling for life in the water, and, when he has reached ground, encumbers him with help? The notice which you have been pleased to take of my labors, had it been early, had been kind; but is has been delayed... til I am known, and do not want it.*
>
> *Your Lordship's most humble, most obedient servant.*

This is a perfect example of why artists should always keep moving forward without depending on patrons, agents, managers, or anyone else but themselves when it comes to their careers. Rarely does anyone want to help a struggling artist until they have proven that they are capable of helping themselves. Most artists throughout history who were able to secure patrons were the ones who were the best networkers and marketers. Being a great artist does help, but that's only part of why many successful artists became so successful. Most of their success happened because they were simply the best networkers and marketers. If you've ever looked at talented artists and wondered why they aren't rich and famous or looked at less talented ones who are, there's your answer.

Poets in King Charles's day knew they had to be good marketers if they wanted to attract his attention. They knew how to play the game and were great at socializing. Often poets would dedicate poems to certain aristocrats or patrons in the hopes of getting more funding or work. They knew that these people also had huge egos and they played into it. Looks like nothing has changed in over 700 years.

In some periods, artists had no creative freedom, and in other periods artists had a lot of creative freedom. But creative freedom usually went hand in hand with economic freedom, and like today, the more well-known the artist was, the more money and creative freedom they had. In Ancient Rome artists weren't hired just because of their talent. They were treated like second-class citizens. In the late Roman Republic the artists started getting more freedom. And in Greece, artists were treated like manual laborers. The patron wanted to get all of the praise.

A painting in the Middle Ages was valuable because of what it was made of, not by who painted it. Blue (made from Lapis Lazuli) and gold in a painting meant that it was more valuable because it came from precious and semi-precious stones. Yellow, green or red paint were made from minerals that came from local sources and weren't as expensive as blue, which had to be imported. Some patrons chose pure gold if they could afford it. The materials could either express certain religious beliefs or promote the level of wealth or status the patron had. The contract specified how much the artist would be paid, how long it would take to finish the project, what kind of materials would be used, and what the subject matter would be. Usually painters accepted all the risks of production so they had to make sure they were covering such expenses as creating and delivering their works. Often the final payment was not made until well after the work was completed and delivered.[2]

Today a painting is valuable for a number of reasons. One reason it could be valuable is because of the person who painted it. Andy Warhol could paint on a pizza box and it would still be valuable. Picasso's first drawing in crayons in a coloring book would be worth millions. Another reason it might have value is because of something called "provenance," or, who owned the painting before. Rothko's "White Center," which last sold for over $72 million to Qatar's ruling family, used to be owned by the Rockefellers. Single family owners of undiscovered paintings are also valuable.

Art can also go up in price because someone at an auction really wants the painting, whether someone owned it before or not, maybe to round out a collection or for personal reasons. So those people find themselves bidding up the price, which may not even be what the painting is worth. Also, where the artwork has been exhibited before can drive up the price. A museum show that is well known and influential can be great exposure for an artist and drive up the price of their work. Collectors who might not have heard of the artist, or liked the artist, may suddenly be interested in their work after seeing it displayed at a prominent museum.

The quality of a painting could affect its price. Paintings that are well maintained and in good condition are of greater value. Paintings that have scratches, blemishes, cracks, and discoloration lose some of their value. And the fact that a painting might have

---

2 See Michelle O'Malley, *The Business of Art: Contracts and the Commissioning Process in Renaissance Italy*, New Haven, CT: Yale University Press, 2005.

been restored affects it. You also want to make sure the painting has durability and will hold its value. A painting of high quality that creates an emotional impact may have a higher value. A popular and important artist can drive up the price of a painting, especially if the artist is a luxury brand with an aura of exclusivity. The BBC documentary "The World's Most Expensive Paintings" explores this practice.

Before the Renaissance, artists were considered skilled laborers, like tradesmen, brick masons, and carpenters. All artists started out as humble apprentices who learned and sharpened their craft in the dingy backrooms of their master's workshop. Quite often they would spend their time sweeping floors and running errands. Before there were schools to teach artists, they learned from their master. They would slowly work their way up the ladder, and once they achieved the level of a master, they were able to branch out on their own and hopefully open their own workshops. There are still areas of art that are considered a craft as well as art, like architecture, graphic arts, and illustration. A "patron" commissions what they want, like a particular house or a website, and the artist finishes the job and gets paid.

Theater before the Renaissance was mostly controlled by the church or often by various trade guilds. The performers weren't really professional actors but regular citizens who acted in their spare time. The first professional actor was a man named Thespis. Before Thespis, plays were sung by a chorus instead of having actors play different roles. The chorus members on stage didn't speak to each other. But at one city festival he tried something unique and broke away from the chorus and started speaking to them. This gesture won him first prize in the festival's contest and the namesake of the term for actors… thespian.

After that, audiences hungered for more of the performance that would come to be called acting. Large outdoor theaters sprung up and playwrights wrote for the new, thriving medium. Thespis was also the first actor to create a traveling performing arts tour. He used a cart as a traveling stage, where he performed, while musicians played in the background. He also invented the theatrical mask to play different roles, which he carried around with him on the road, along with props and makeup. In 1939 a branch of the National Theater of Greece sponsored a tour of "The Wagon of Thespis."[3]

As the art and craft of acting began to develop, so did the clash between the amateurs and the new professional actors. Acting became an actual profession during the Elizabethan period. Patronage for actors began after the Act of 1545, which stated that anyone who wasn't a member of a guild could be arrested for vagrancy. To keep from being arrested, actors would find important patrons to "sponsor" them. This meant that they would technically be their servant and avoid being locked up for vagrancy. The patron-actor relationship in many of these cases was just for show, but some of them did help the actors out financially.

Before the Renaissance, musicians, like most artists of the time, primarily were hired by churches and courts. The music in churches was usually sung by soloists, but after the Renaissance it was sung by a male choir. The patronage of music eventually shifted to the courts, where kings, dukes, and princes would compete for the best musicians and composers money could buy. Even the artists who had patrons couldn't just create whatever they wanted and put it up for sale like they can now. They were paid to create what their patrons wanted them to create, which often meant they wanted themselves painted into the commissioned art. That meant they had total control over the art. And the patrons who put their money into art also helped steer the culture, much like today.

There were Renaissance versions of "American Idol" or "America's Got Talent" where patrons would sponsor competitions to encourage artists to create their best work possible. Just like

---

3 http://www.lookandlearn.com/blog/5324/a-history-of-the-theatre/

"American Idol" competitors, such as Jennifer Hudson, sometimes the losers went on to greater fame than the winners. Like today, there was even a bit of competition between the patrons to commission the best artwork and hire the most talented artists they could find. Artists of the Renaissance were the first entrepreneurial artists, and it was the beginning of consumerism in the art world.

Today, museums are courting the next generation of art patrons. Some of these are the nouveau riche and some are the children of wealthy baby boomers who have been the lifeblood of museum patronage for the past few decades. But the new generation may not follow in the footsteps of their parents. Or they may not donate as generously as their parents. They have different priorities as far as philanthropy goes, and they have plenty of charities they can donate to.

In the past, wealthy families like the Gettys and the Rockefellers would donate a large amount of money to museums and not ask about their return on investment. Today, that is more of an issue, with the new generation concerned about how that money will be put to use. If today's museums start to suffer from lack of funding, some may find themselves in a bind. And when any industry that hires or buys product from artists goes through budget constraints, all artists suffer, and eventually so does the public. We usually think about art today as something an artist paints and then tries to sell on the open market. This is art that the artist wants to create for themselves or sometimes with the audience in mind. But plenty of art today is still commissioned.

During the Renaissance, when the middle class had plenty of disposable income, more artists were working, and the new art patrons were commissioning them to paint portraits and other subjects that suited their fancy. Merchants were thriving and needed to hire artists to paint their stores. They also hired artists to sing, dance, play music, and juggle outside their stores to attract more customers.

Another period in history when the middle class had lots of

disposable income was during the Industrial Revolution. Demand for labor increased the demand for art, which meant more artists were working. With the rise of the middle class, high art for just the elite now had competition. The middle class was suddenly able to change the art culture to suit their own interests. Today the middle class is a class of art patrons we normally don't think about when it comes to commissioning art. But there is actually a big segment of the population who is doing just that.

People commission art for all kinds of reasons. Maybe they want a one of a kind piece that you can't get anywhere else. They want it to be unique and special. Some people like the feeling of being involved with an artist in the creative process, especially if they aren't creative themselves. They can say that they had a hand in the process. This is one reason many people donate to crowdfunding. Some people simply like the idea of supporting an artist whose work they admire. And if you want to give someone a gift they will always remember, a commissioned piece of art that reminds them of you is a perfect way of doing it. A commissioned art piece is also an investment that will bring you joy for years to come. People who commission artists are truly modern day art patrons.

There is a website called Masters of Portrait Art that features several of America's finest portrait artists. They have painted portraits of presidents, kings, prime ministers, and other world leaders. Corporations will often commission an artist to paint a portrait of the CEO to hang on the wall of the company's lobby other prominent area. A university might commission a portrait of the university's founder, and high ranking military leaders also may have portraits done of them.

Commissioned pet art is very popular with pet owners, either for their living pets or the ones who have passed on as a memorial. Artists from websites like Dog & Cat Art or The Creative Cat will study pictures of your animals and recreate a portrait from them that is completely unique and customized just for you. Another website that deals with commissioned art is called Ugallery. You pick the artist, the style, the colors, and the price range. You have over 500 artists to choose from, and you arrange your collaboration with the artist. This allows anyone to own original artwork that fits their needs. Instead of dealing with a middleman, Ugallery cuts out the middleman and streamlines the process for both artist and patron.

This is no different than hiring a graphic designer to do a book cover, advertisement, CD, website art, or logo design. The artist is still being hired on commission to create a piece of art for the customer, who becomes their patron. Web developer and artist Steve Gadlin took on commissioned art in a unique way when he appeared on the TV show "Shark Tank" with a new idea called "I Want to Draw a Cat For You." The pitch was that for $9.95 he would draw a stick figure cartoon cat that is originally designed just for you. Shark Mark Cuban went in business with him for $25,000 for one-third ownership. The quirky business raked in over $200,000 the first year. Now he's added hand drawn greeting cards and a customized song section called "I'll Write a Song For You."

Today, the public decides what art is and what they like, which is all over the map. There are niches for just about any kind of art you can think of, and that creates more markets for artists, even if that market is a small one. Just like in the Renaissance, art flourishes when people have disposable income. The more people with disposable income, the more artists will be employed, and the more patrons we will have in general, whether it's the wealthy, big corporations, the public, or small businesses.

Patronage for the arts has always been very unpredictable. It continually fluctuates according to changes in the economy, state and federal tax laws, culture, and audience tastes, and through changing opportunities for a broader spectrum of sponsorship of artists, such as crowdfunding, foundation grants, corporate sponsorship, and micro-sponsorship.

How Clowns Escaped the Death Penalty in Ancient Rome

Censorship and Art Patronage

"Whoever controls the media controls the mind"

Jim Morrison

THERE'S NO DENYING that art and the artists that create it help shape the world around them. But what happens when those artists are censored? Censorship has been around since the early Roman days. Those in power believed that morality and the character of the citizens needed to be kept in check. They believed the ideas and values of society had to be controlled.

Therefore they needed someone to assume the role of censor. The Roman censor had a huge amount of responsibility. Not only were they in charge of maintaining the census and overseeing certain aspects of government finances, but they were also the ones in charge of supervising public morality. And that included the art that was created, whether it was fine art or performing art.

Censorship has always existed in every society throughout

history. There is a constant clash between what one person views as offensive and another views as art. A lot has also depended on who was in power at the time and what their political, religious, and ideological views were. Under the US Constitution, obscenity and certain types of speech aren't protected, and, for a time, artistic expression was also not recognized as being a form of speech that should be constitutionally protected. [4]

One of the earliest and most famous examples of art censorship was the case of Socrates, one of the fathers of Western philosophy and a well-known public speaker. His phrase "the unexamined life is not worth living" sums up the motto that Socrates lived by. He became a martyr for free speech, which would lie dormant in history for the next 2000 years. We aren't able to read Socrates's words because he never wrote anything down. But through the words written by his contemporaries and students, we can understand why his teachings are still important today. Those teachings were the basis of his trial, and ultimate forced suicide, when he was convicted by a jury of his peers for corrupting the youth of Athens and for failing to accept the gods that were acknowledged by the city of Athens.

Some would say that Socrates's crime was that he questioned everything in great detail. His irony and wit didn't always sit well with his enemies, who were often challenged to a debate. And suddenly the man who had always spoken his mind freely was forced to drink poison Hemlock at the age of seventy, being silenced forever. Unlike many people at that time Socrates was unmaterialistic and preached finding the good in life and in other human beings. He didn't just want to talk about the world around him, he wanted to actually change it.

It's interesting that one of Socrates's best students was Plato, a former playwright, who seemed to have a love-hate relationship

----

4 Marjorie Heins, *Sex, Sin, and Blasphemy: A Guide to America's Censorship Wars,* New York, NY: The New Press, 1993, 5.

with the arts and was a staunch defender of censorship. Even as his beloved teacher was being executed for his beliefs, Plato was fighting to censor what playwrights and poets wrote. He felt that art had the power to stir emotions and persuade people and therefore was dangerous. Whether it was music, dance, painting, or poetry, it all had the potential to be dangerous. He felt that it threatened society, and in order to have an ideal society, the arts had to be strictly controlled. He was more interested in how it would affect society as a whole than about personal freedom of expression. In contrast, the playwright Euripides believed in artists having freedom of speech, but his play *Hippolytus* was shouted down by an angry audience because the character Phaedra had romantic feelings for her stepson.

Throughout history, artists have both needed patronage and have, at the same time, been restrained by it. During the Julio-Claudian dynasty there was the illusion that artists had freedom of expression. But sometimes that wasn't the case. During Emperor Augustus's reign, he ordered a sweep of all books that he felt were intended to defame him or his supporters. Any such books were to be rounded up and burned in public in Rome.

Included in those were the books of Titus Labienus, an orator and historian. Titus got the nickname "rabid one" because his books were so full of controversial material that when he recited them in public he would skip over big chunks of dialogue and insist that they were to be read after his death. He viciously attacked different classes of Roman society as a historian. The punishment for a writer that spoke out against the state was burning of either one or all of their books. Augustus made sure all of Titus's books were burned, though some of Titus's writings were saved from the fire by his loyal friends and fellow scholars. They risked their lives to get them out. When Caligula came into power in 37 CE, he thought that it would be better if the writing was available for future reference and he reversed the rulings of Augustus.

Freedom of speech and freedom of expression really became a problem after the invention of the printing press in 1455. It was a threat to religion and politics because writings could now be mass produced. Religious censorship, against anything the church found to be offensive or dangerous, came first followed by political censorship when Martin Luther defied the Pope. Luther's "Ninety Five Theses" was condemned in 1517 by Pope Leo X. Then Emperor Charles V banned the printing, possession, reading, sale, or copying of all of Luther's books.

In 1543 the Catholic Church decreed that no book could be printed or sold without their permission. They also controlled all universities and what was allowed to be read. Similar to what happened to Titus under Augustus, in 1564 the papacy banned books that they felt Catholics shouldn't read. They even banned authors whose work they deemed to be too offensive and threatening to the political and moral order of society. Now censorship was enforced on all fronts. Phillip II of Spain, for one, established the Peruvian Inquisition. He had officers examining books at ports and in libraries, printing houses, and bookstores. This included the burning of the Mayan Codices, which destroyed a big part of Mayan cultural heritage and literature.

Even the postal service has served as a censor of sorts, especially in times of war. It's easy to forget how important the postal service has been in its advancement of communication. After the postal service was first established in France in 1464, it became the primary way that printed material was distributed. In 1865 the first federal law controlling distribution of obscene materials through the mail was enacted in the United States. This was then expanded through the Comstock Act and was amended to include the word "indecent."

Under this law, some literary classics by the following writers were censored:

- Ernest Hemingway

- George Bernard Shaw
- D.H. Lawrence
- James Joyce
- Henry Miller
- Sigmund Freud
- Margaret Mead
- Leo Tolstoy

Even today, the mailing of certain offensive material, including books, magazines, and films, is still regulated by the postal service.

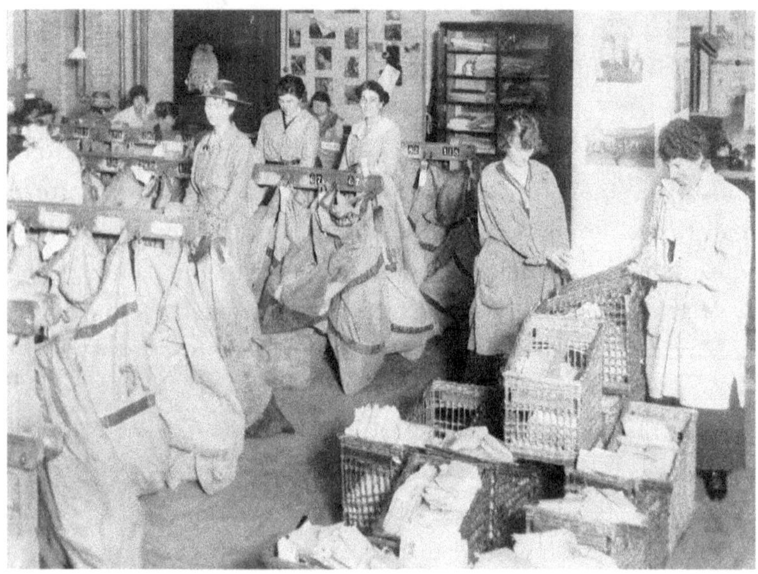

Books, and other printed materials, are still being banned today. In the United States, most book banning is usually done on a local level, not federal. Communities do their own censoring, especially in schools and libraries. The Library of Congress, the world's largest repository of information and knowledge, put on an exhibition entitled "Books That Shaped America," that included some books that had been banned at one time:

- *The Adventures of Huckleberry Finn* by Mark Twain – In 1885 it was banned for being "trash and suitable only for the slums" according to the librarians in Concord, Massachusetts who banned it shortly after its publication. It's still one of the most challenged and banned books of all time and remains in the top 20 on the list.
- *Beloved* by Toni Morrison – The book is often challenged by parents for its violence and sexual content.
- *The Call of the Wild* by Jack London – The book is challenged for being dark and violent. It was banned in Italy, Yugoslavia, and Nazi Germany.
- *The Grapes of Wrath* by John Steinbeck – It was banned in Kern County, California, for profanity and sexual references. It was also banned in Italy and Turkey.

In Cold Blood by Truman Capote – It was banned for having too much sex, violence, and profanity, but it was later removed from the ban.

Even *Little Red Riding Hood* was once censored because she was bringing wine to Grandma as a gift. *Alice's Adventures in Wonderland* was also banned at one time because the animal characters were able to speak like humans, and some people objected to that. Los Angeles, in 1929, banned all of the Tarzan books because he was living in the jungle with Jane without being married. In 1959 there was also a big public outcry to ban *Lady Chatterley's Lover*.

And it wasn't just writing that was censored. In the years between 1642 and 1660, Puritans in England passed laws to drive out what they called "sinful" theater. For one thing, theaters were used for other purposes like gambling and bear baiting. The Globe Theater attracted huge crowds of mostly young people, gamblers, beggars, thieves, and pick-pockets. The citizens of London agreed with the Puritans and worried about the rise in crime it was creating.

The government decided that plays had to be regulated because playwrights were using the stage to express their own views on politics and religion. In an effort to suppress freedom of speech and avoid any criticism of the crown, they required all plays to be registered prior to publication. Theatrical performances were suspended for five years. Then, after the law expired, another law passed by Oliver Cromwell's government declared all actors were to be considered rogues. They were to be seized and whipped, and anyone caught attending a play was to be fined.

Today, theater performances can still be censored, as the musical *Oh! Calcutta!* discovered. The nude musical was a smash hit off-Broadway. But when the show was taken on the road, it ran into trouble in Chattanooga, Tennessee. The city enforced laws against public nudity because it was taking place in a public theater.

But this is nothing compared to Belarus where actors can literally find themselves in prison or even subjected to violence and oppression simply by being onstage. In 1990, Belarus declared their independence from the Soviet Union. In 1994 it became a dictatorial regime, and suddenly all aspects of the citizens' lives were controlled, including their freedom of speech and expression. The state controls all of the media and security forces are used to silence dissenting voices.

In 2005, dramatist Natalia Koliada, her playwright husband Nikolai Khalezin, and director Vladimir Scherban started the Belarus Free Theater as a way to express their anger and dissatisfaction with the totalitarian regime. Members of the Free Theater are forced to perform in secret, using apartments and houses as their stages. To accommodate larger audiences, they perform in the forest. To attend a performance you have to call a special phone number, then you're put on a waiting list and alerted right before the performance by email or text. All precautions are taken to avoid detection by the state, yet performances have been raided by the security forces, and everyone present, including young children, have been arrested and detained. The theater has strong support from patrons and playwrights such as Tom Stoppard and Harold Pinter. Pinter allows them to perform his plays without paying royalties. The Belarus Free Theater members have vowed to continue to operate until the people of Belarus and freedom of speech are free again.

✍

There is an old saying: "in humor there is truth." That's why the royalty would hire court jesters, because they were the voice of reason. Most cultures throughout history have had clowns, and the ones who acted as court jesters had the greatest freedom of speech. They were usually the only ones who could speak out against the government, and because of their openness and frankness they would often affect government policy. While others would have been thrown in prison, the clown was spared and could openly speak their mind.

The 17th century playwright Moliere once said, "The purpose of comedy is to correct the vices of men. I see no reason why anyone should be exempt." Obviously, not everyone agrees on what is funny and what isn't, but because something is written under the category of comedy, it seems to get less censorship. You can get away with being cruel as long as it's funny.

Music has also been censored throughout history. In fact, music is considered so powerful that many government leaders have felt that it could lead to cultural and political revolutions. But some leaders used it to their advantage, like Hitler, who strongly believed that young people should join singing groups because they were a way of building a more obedient youth population.

Musicians who lived under Hitler's rule were strictly monitored and had to fit within certain standards approved by the Fuhrer whose favorite composers were Richard Wagner, Ludwig van Beethoven, and Anton Bruckner. But the Nazis also wanted to appease the German people, so limited artistic freedom was allowed. Jewish and Russian musicians were banned from concert halls, but Hitler would listen to their music in private.

Many musicians during that time were forced to make a deal with the devil. As long as they were allowed to play their music, they were willing to ignore the evil. Well-known Jewish musicians like Otto Klemperer and Bruno Walter were either forced to quit or they quit on their own. But another well-known violinist, German-born conductor and composer Adolf Busch, refused to play under those circumstances. Many of his friends were Jewish, including Karl Doktor, the violist for his quartet, and the idea of playing without him was unacceptable. He left Germany, vowing never to return as long as Hitler was in power. He was the first non-Jewish classical musician to leave Germany on a matter of principal in protesting Hitler's actions.

Though the quartet came to the United States, and his friend was able to get a job, Adolf spent years eking out a living; his days of being a rich and famous violinist were over. Yet the Adolph Busch Foundation now grants $10,000 annually to an organization chosen by the Board of Advisors. Sometimes additional organizations are also awarded and their mission statement says it all: "Our mission is to recognize and support organizations that use music to promote a more civil and just society." Busch's story has been told in *Adolf Busch: The Life of an Honest Musician.*[5]

Music censorship is still such a problem around the world that an organization called FreeMuse was formed to address it. According to their website, FreeMuse is "an independent international membership organization advocating and defending freedom of expression for musicians and composers worldwide." FreeMuse was formed during the first World Conference on Music and Censorship in 1998. Professionals came together to discuss censorship issues. Some have been minor and some extreme, but all infringed on the musical artist's freedom of expression. And artists around the world have faced punishment through censorship of their art.

Ahmad Tor Zahir was an Afghan singer, songwriter, and composer. He was well known and was sometimes called "The King of

---

5 Tully Potter, *Adolph Busch: The Life of an Honest Musician*, London, UKL Toccata Classics.

Afghan Music." His songs were based on Dari poems and are sung in Dari, Pashto, and English. Many of his songs were critical of the Afghan government who destroyed a lot of them. He produced thirty albums in his young life, all of them live recordings made forty years ago without the aid of more modern sound technology. He was killed on his 33rd birthday. How he died is still a mystery, but his family believes it had something to do with his criticism of the government.

Pashtun singer Ghazala Javed rose from poverty to become a well-loved singing star in Afghanistan. But she knew she would always live in fear because of her chosen profession. The Pashtuns love music, but shun singers, dancers, and musicians as immoral people doing the devil's work. The day she died she had an eerie premonition, which proved to be true. She always knew she had to worry about the Taliban as they would kill musicians simply for being musicians. They had banned singing and dancing, along with TV and music, for being disrespectful and sacrilegious. After leaving her hairdresser, she was gunned down, along with her father. The singer with the voice of an angel is just as popular, if not more popular, today.

Afghan singer Mariam says she has been verbally and physically attacked in the streets for singing. Yet she keeps on doing it, even though she knows that it puts her life in danger. She was the first female singer, after the fall of the Taliban in 2001, to sing in public. In 2004 more restrictions on dancing and music were lifted after the new regime change. A reality TV show aired in Afghanistan in 2005 called "Afghan Star" that was the equivalent to "America's Got Talent" or "The Voice." For the first season more than 1,000 hopefuls auditioned for their chance to become vocal celebrities. In 2009 a documentary was released about the show's third season.

Iranian-born rapper Shahin Najafi has been on the run, hiding in safe houses, after receiving two fatwas, or death threats, for insulting a 9th-century imam and criticizing the corrupt regime of Tehran. Shahin knows that he is a marked man and can't perform live. There is a $100,000 bounty on his head for anyone who kills him. Shahin is now a German citizen and is a rock star there. His fans feel that the mullahs have deprived him of his free speech, even though he is in Germany. The regime wants to silence him because the subjects he sings about, such as homophobia, drug addiction, and censorship, are taboo.

Chinese artist Ai Weiwei was put under house arrest for his political activism and for speaking out against the Chinese government. Weiwei's family was sent to a labor camp when he was a year old. After the end of the Cultural Revolution, his family moved to Beijing, where he enrolled in the Beijing Film Academy and studied animation. He briefly studied in New York City and delved deeper into avant-garde art. Once he moved back to Beijing he started a blog, which became quite popular with his fans but very unpopular with the Chinese government. His visual art, which included woodworking, video, and photography, was considered obscene and pornographic. He was locked up for tax evasion and subjected to psychological torture while he was imprisoned. But he continues to fight for the rights of artists and other Chinese people to enjoy free speech.

Hugely successful Burmese comedian Zarganar was sentenced to fifty-nine years in prison for making fun of the Burmese government and exposing their crimes and human rights violations. He was already banned from performing when a documentary filmmaker secretly interviewed him for a film about freedom of artistic expression. In 2011 he received amnesty as his country tries to move forward towards an uncertain future. Just as the satirists did back in ancient Rome, Zarganar uses satire to speak out against tyranny and oppression, constantly pushing the envelope against government censorship.

Award winning poet and journalist Aron Atabek has been in a Kazakhstan prison since 2007, and most of that time has been spent in solitary confinement in extremely harsh conditions. Atabek was the founder of a monthly newspaper called *The Truth* and has authored nine books. His imprisonment turned into a nightmare following the online publication of "The Heart of Eurasia," a scathing critique of President Nursultan Nazarbayev's autocratic regime, which Atabek wrote in prison and had smuggled out. He's been in solitary confinement, denied access to natural light, any writing materials, and phone calls. Like many places around the world, independent voices are not tolerated in Kazakhstan.

Radio has also been a target for censorship. Like the mass printing of books, it can reach a very large audience. The regulation of publicly-owned radio set a precedence for newer technology such as television and the internet. In 1926 the government body that regulated radio was called the Federal Radio Commission or the FRC. In 1927 Congress passed the Radio Act that granted federal regulators censorship authority over the airwaves. And in 1934 Congress created the Federal Communications Commission, which replaced the Federal Radio Commission, to regulate publicly-owned bandwidth.

According to the Federal Communications Commission's website, obscene programming of any kind is a violation of the law. Indecent programming or profane language during specific hours is also a violation of the law: "The FCC may revoke a station license, impose a monetary forfeiture or issue a warning if a station airs obscene, indecent or profane material." So exactly what do they consider obscene material? There are three objectives that must be met:

- An average person applying contemporary community standards must find that the material, as a whole, appeals to the prurient interest.
- The material must depict or describe, in a patently offensive way, sexual conduct specifically defined by applicable law.
- The material, taken as a whole, must lack serious literary, artistic, political, or scientific value.

In 1970, Grateful Dead's lead singer Jerry Garcia did a profanity-laced interview on a radio station, and the station was slapped with a $100 fine. George Carlin's seven dirty words routine was also considered obscene, and a radio station that aired it was fined by the FCC. Charlie Wakler, a colorful and popular radio personality in South Carolina in the '60s, was known for his raunchy stories and thinly-veiled double meanings. He would often use the phrase "let it all hang out," which the FCC cracked down on as being obscene and indecent. But radio shock jock Howard Stern took it to a whole new level when he racked up more than a million dollars in indecency fines. He eventually landed on Sirius Satellite Radio, a subscription-based radio service that is exempt from FCC regulation. The FCC doesn't monitor the airwaves on a consistent basis but usually waits until they get enough complaints from the public before making a move. Then they will investigate and take action.

The government of the People's Republic of China constantly monitors and blocks the airwaves by radio jamming, the process of transmitting radio signals on the same frequency as the intended target. They disrupt shortwave radio communications by broadcasting music, drumming, or other noise, such as Chinese folk music known as The Firedrake, using shortwave broadcasting equipment. Most foreign broadcasters are jammed by the Communist Party, such as the BBC and Voice of America, but there are also Chinese broadcasters that are banned. Attempts have been made by foreign broadcasters to come up with censorship-circumvention software so that Chinese audiences can listen online.

⁓

Censorship becomes a slippery slope argument. One person's view of obscenity can be quite different from the next person's view. Freedom of expression faced another large hurdle with the introduction of celluloid. Like mass produced books, films were seen as a threat because they were the first visual and aural mass media. For the first fifty years of their existence they were also the most popular and big threats when it came to censorship. Many cities and states had their own movie censorship boards in the 1930s-50s who would pre-screen films and ban those that they considered inappropriate.[6]

In Harvard scholar Ben Urwand's book *The Collaboration: Hollywood's Pact With Hitler*, there are claims that Hollywood studio executives, such as Louis B. Meyer of MGM, worked with Hitler's censors to alter films so they could protect access to the German film market, the world's second largest at the time. Hitler threatened to ban over 250 movies if the studios didn't agree to his edits. The film *All Quiet on the Western Front* was banned in Germany because of its portrayal of Germans. It was heavily edited afterwards. Other films that showed Germany in a bad light were never even produced.

As soon as movies started even going in the direction of any sex or violence the "morality police" started forcing them to reign it in. In response to that, film industry executives decided to start regulating themselves with a production code. Because of the hard economic times, it made sense from a money standpoint to self-censor and save the extra money that would have gone into reediting the film. The code was actually pretty strict and prohibited nudity, drug use, suggestive dancing, offensive words, ridicule of the clergy, scenes of actual childbirth, and brutal killings. It even went so far as to say that the sanctity of marriage be upheld, and plots couldn't sympathize with criminals.

This stayed in place from the 1930s to the 1960s and was a way for the movie industry to stave off any government intervention. In the late 1950s through 1968, the code started weakening due to the impact of foreign films, TV, daring directors who pushed the envelope, and intervention from the courts. Moviemakers would back down on their self-censorship promise and start making movies that went well beyond what they agreed to censor. So the Hollywood Production Code Administration was formed to strictly enforce the

---

6 Heins, *Sex, Sin and Blasphemy*, 11.

code. They fined any theater that ran a film without the PCA seal of approval $25,000.

In 1968 the code was replaced by the MPAA age-based ratings system that exists today. The documentary *This Film is Not Yet Rated* sets out to find the people who were responsible for rating films. Jack Valenti, the man who has overseen the MPAA for decades, has always kept the names of the raters secret. Filmmakers may get turned down for a rating but not be told why or what they need to change.

Here is how the ratings break down:

G – General Audience: no nudity, no sex, no drugs, violence must be cartoonish and minimal

PG – Parental Guidance: strong language, brief nudity, light violence

PG-13 – Parents Strongly Cautioned: stronger language, violence, and nudity

R – Restricted: no children seventeen or under without parent or guardian, sexual themes, frank sex talk, strong violence

NC-17 – No children seventeen or under at all

Throughout history certain films, from a number of different countries, have been completely banned for a variety of reasons. In some countries a film can be shown but only after the director agrees to have it edited down to their specifications. Here is a list of some of the banned films:

- *Rambo* – Banned in Burma for negative portrayals of Burmese soldiers
- *Farewell My Concubine* – Chinese film banned for homosexual themes and negative portrayal of Communism
- *Monty Python's Life of Brian* – Banned in Norway because the jokes may be offensive to religious people
- *Apocalypse Now* – Banned in South Korea for its anti-war theme

- *Anna and the King* – Banned in Thailand because it might be disrespectful towards the King of Thailand
- *Dirty Harry* – Banned in Finland for glamorizing police brutality
- *Liar Liar* – Banned in Iran for showing that adultery is legal
- *Zoolander* – Banned in Iran because it is seen as supporting gay rights
- *Fahrenheit 9/11* – Banned in Iraq because of a scene where Saddam Hussein is burning in hell
- *Prophecies of Nostradamus* – Banned in Japan due to a scene where a research party is attacked by radioactive cannibals and a pair of deformed, post-apocalyptic mutants fight over a worm
- *The Evil Dead* – Banned in Singapore due to extreme graphic violence and gore
- *Up in Smoke* – Banned in South Africa for fear that it might inspire kids to start smoking pot
- *The Grapes of Wrath* – Banned under Stalin because it showed that even the poorest Americans could afford a car, unlike in the Soviet Union
- *Pink Flamingos* – Banned in Turkey for extreme nudity
- *Barney's Great Adventure* – Banned in Malaysia for being unacceptable for children

It isn't just governments who want to put their foot down about an artist or a piece of art they find objectionable. Corporate brands who spend good money funding artists often have to walk a fine line between letting artists use their own creativity and protecting their brand name.

The Musee de L'Elysee was caught in the middle of just such a predicament in 2011. The Lacoste Elysee Prize is a prestigious international photography contest where the artists are encouraged to interpret the theme of the contest in any way they want. But when

Palestinian artist Larrissa Sansour entered her photography exhibit entitled "Nation Estate" in the contest, Lacoste decided to exclude her entry, which was inspired by Palestine's attempt to gain UN recognition. The museum stated that they stood by the artists' freedom of speech and planned to show the exhibit themselves.

Another form of censorship has nothing to do with the artist's work but with the inclusion of another competing sponsor's brand in a painting, photography exhibit, play, or any other kind of art project. An interdisciplinary festival called "Transmission LA" was presented at L.A's Museum of Contemporary Art and featured the work of sixteen contemporary artists, musicians, filmmakers, and designers. It was curated by Mike D, formally of the Beastie Boys, and was sponsored by Mercedes-Benz. The evening included a concert and the international debut of the Mercedes-Benz Concept Style Coupe.

Artist Chris Silva's piece was projected on the wall in a segment entitled "Bring Your Own Beamer" (not beamer as in BMW but beamer meaning slide projector). The segment was intended to show how audio and visual art forms can complement each other. His project happened to contain a model of a 2010 Peugeot race car. He left the project, and when he came back there was a postcard taped over the lens. When he tried to fix it, he was approached by one of the organizers and asked to remove it. He was told that Mercedes-Benz wasn't happy about the piece. After all, they were footing the bill for the event and didn't want the competitor's brand shown.

The largest retailer in the world, Walmart, sells more music than any retailer in the United States. Walmart also exercises a tremendous amount of censorship over what kind of music they sell. Since Walmart is a private company, they can legally sell whatever kind of music they want to sell. Cover art and even lyrics have been changed to suit the corporation. The lyrics of the song "Rape Me" by Nirvana were changed to "Waif Me.' Cover art designs by John Mellencamp, the Black Crowes, and White Zombies were changed in order to be sold in Walmart.

Jane's Addiction's *Nothing's Shocking* album cover, created by front man Perry Farrell, features a sculpture of a pair of nude female conjoined twins with their heads on fire. Farrell hired the employees of Warner Bros. to create the cover sculpture, and after learning how to create the sculptures himself by closely watching them, he fired them and created his own artwork. When retailers objected to the album's cover and nine out of the eleven leading record store chains refused to carry *Nothing's Shocking*, the record had to be issued covered with plain brown paper.

Album covers have been banned for other reasons too, like violence. Pink Floyd's *Wish You Were Here* album showed two men shaking hands in an alley, one was on fire. Some retailers thought it was too violent and refused to carry it in their stores. Other reasons for banning or changing album covers have included copyright infringement or glorifying smoking. Walmart also refuses to sell CDs with parental warning stickers on them, saying "The goal is not to eliminate the need for parents to review the merchandise their children buy. The policy simply helps eliminate the most objectionable material from Wal-Mart's shelves."[7]

Sheryl Crow refused to change part of the lyrics to "Love is a Good Thing" that included the phrase "Watch our children while they kill each other with a gun they bought at Walmart discount stores." Walmart refused to sell it. In 2009 when the band Green Day released their album *21st Century Breakdown* they refused to sell it to Walmart, after the retail giant asked them to censor it to make it more family friendly. Three years later, with the release of *Uno! Dos! Tre!* they did a complete turnaround and decided to clean it up in order to make it acceptable for Walmart stores. They actually went into the studio and recorded two completely different versions of some of the songs.

---

7 PBS News Hour -https://www.pbs.org/newshour/economy/
  business-july-dec04-wal-mart_08-20.

The director's cut of Oliver Stone's movie *Natural Born Killers* was banned from both Wal-Mart and Kmart. Movie studios are even hesitant to release a film with an NC-17 rating because many of the big box chain stores won't carry them. Directors have been shooting alternate versions of their films for years so they can be shown on TV or in different markets.

Today the US Constitution protects our freedom of speech, but censorship in the arts, even in the United States still exists. One thing many artists worry about when getting sponsorship is whether their work will be censored. Censorship usually isn't a problem for artists looking for sponsorship because both parties agree on the project up front, and few corporations are going to sponsor something socially or morally controversial. Artists will often self-censor out of fear of losing their sponsors or upsetting the public. But they also have the freedom to choose whichever sponsor they want to work with.

So, should artists be worried about corporate censorship? My personal opinion would be "no" because as an artist you should only align yourself with companies who share your artistic vision. There are corporations out there who will support controversial art. That's especially true with smaller businesses and start-ups. That's the great thing about sponsorship—there is a sponsor out there for every artist, no matter what kind of art you produce.

Museums used to get their funding from the government and individuals. But museums today who are being squeezed by budget constraints are having to turn to corporate sponsorship in order to get some of the exhibits they really want. One such case was a recent Bank of America sponsorship of "The Wyeths: Three Generations" for the Montclair Art Museum. Bank of America did choose the works, but the museum also had a say in their installation.

Corporations are "likely to fund museums whose programs attract large middle-class audiences and exhibits that have good PR value…. Corporations often sponsor theme exhibitions that reflect their brands, like Horse and Man, sponsored by Polo/Ralph Lauren,

Undercover Agents, a lingerie exhibit, sponsored by Victoria's Secret, or toy exhibits, sponsored by Fischer-Price."[8]

Public school systems are facing similar issues to museums. They have long resisted corporate sponsorship and the idea of selling out to the highest bidder. But with shrinking budgets, many are hard-pressed to offer the kind of education and entertainment for the kids that they would like to have. Corporate sponsors have stepped in to help by sponsoring speakers or other types of entertainers and by brandishing their corporate logo on a football field.

One such example is the grocery store chain Shop Rite in Brooklawn, New Jersey. Shop Rite has pledged $100,000 over the next twenty years to the school, in addition to donating food for needy families and the hiring of special education needs students at the local grocery stores. In exchange, the Shop Rite name and logo is prominently placed on the new gym. But the corporation doesn't push any curriculum ideas on the school or ask for special favors.

As we saw in the Introduction, Charles Mee was able to find a lifetime patron who allowed him to write whatever he wanted with no restrictions, and Jean Noel was also able to write her book with no restrictions. If an artist is worried about eventually losing their sponsorship because of being censored or for any other reason, then it would be a good idea to have more than one sponsor. In fact, having a portfolio of sponsors is the best way to guarantee you can keep working uninterrupted as a sponsored artist.

The bottom line is that the person who pays the bills will get to decide if a piece is censored or not. It's their decision to sponsor and it's the artist's decision to take their money… or not.

---

8 Rosanne Martorella, *Art and Business: An International Perspective on Sponsorship*, Santa Barbara, CA: Praeger, 1996, 217, 218.

The Church as Art Patron

"For it is in giving that we receive."

Saint Francis of Assisi

Throughout history, art patronage has always been associated with wealth and power. It took a certain amount of money to be able to commission an artist to do a painting or an architect to design a building. The wealthy were those who owned a lot of land. And nobody owned more land back in the early Renaissance than the church.

It's hard to say exactly who the earliest patrons were, but certainly the church was one of the first and one of the biggest. Some of the earliest surviving artworks can be found on the walls of the meeting halls of persecuted Roman Empire Christians. These artworks were painted frescoes of biblical scenes. They weren't just illustrations but were also interpretations of the Bible. This early Christian art was considered neutral and could be enjoyed and accepted by both Christians and pagans.

Medieval art focused on biblical scenes and religious themes.

The Catholic church was the biggest art patron and the main sponsor of architecture, commissioning artists to build and decorate elaborate Gothic cathedrals. A lot of the Gothic architecture that still stands today was built during the Medieval age. The architects were in high demand back then, and they were paid well. Buildings such as churches and cathedrals were an indication of a king's wealth and power. Most of the art that survived after the fall of the Roman Empire is Christian art. Part of the reason is because churches preserved their art.

The Roman Catholic Church was well-funded and commissioned many artists to produce paintings and sculptures that glorified Christianity. Another example is the illuminated manuscript, made with such materials as gold dust, silver, and expensive and rare color pigments. These stunning books were produced by scribes and monks. But the monk-artists who put them together were paid very little money and got little recognition for their hard work. There was quite a disconnect between the vow of poverty the clergy were supposed to take and the extravagant spending of the church.

Art patronage in the Middle Ages was pretty rare as the great pandemic of the Black Death had a profound effect on late Medieval art. An estimated 50-200 million people died during this time period, and art really took a back seat. Most people were simply trying to stay alive. What art was still around reflected the darkness of the time with motifs of death everywhere. Music, art, poetry, plays, and prose were all affected. Writers and philosophers chronicled the horror of living with such a disaster of tremendous magnitude.

But once the plague ended, a new thriving middle class emerged. The bourgeoisie began to invest in art, and some became the new patrons of their time. Only the best of the best of artists were able to secure patronage, either with the king or wealthy nobles. The proliferation of consumer goods was the beginning of what we now call "consumerism." Renaissance artists were the first to take control of the demand for art and use it to their advantage, as more people had greater disposable income.

Italy's geographic location and banking infrastructure left them well-poised for economic growth, outpacing the rest of Europe. Consumer art thrived. Invention and innovation in consumer art was in full swing by the 16th century. Artists competed to capture a bigger market share. Consumers wanted to fill their homes with art of all kinds. And artists were more than willing to keep creating as much art as possible so they could do so. But during the Middle Ages artists were just considered skilled laborers on the same scale as a slave. They didn't associate themselves with anyone from the upper classes. There was no formal training at all, and artists certainly didn't create any kind of art for themselves like they do today.

What did change for some artists towards the later years of the Middle Ages was the introduction of the guilds. During this time in history, few artists were able to strike out on their own and become prosperous. So, many of them joined a guild for their collective power. Certain standards were set for each industry, and artists were able to enjoy a living wage. But individualism went by the wayside. You were appreciated for your willingness to act as a collective, and you were merely a craftsman who worked in a shop that was overseen by a master artist.

To become a master artist one would have to meet certain criteria. Part of that criteria was to complete an apprenticeship in a particular industry under a master artist, become a master of your craft, and pay your dues into the guild. As a member of the bourgeoisie, a master craftsman was entitled to certain rights, such as participation in government and the right to deal in free trade. Only the masters could sell the products they made and were allowed to employ other artists to work for them. During this time a piece of art was known more for what it was made of than the artist who made it. Artists still largely remained anonymous, but they could make a living if they worked for a master. They didn't enjoy any kind of social benefits from being an artist, but that would change during the Renaissance.

There were other artists who played a big part in the Medieval ages: acrobats, jugglers, jesters, singers, and storytellers traveled from town to town, bringing entertainment and much needed revenue to local cities and towns. And actors were important because most people couldn't read, so it was up to the actors to bring history to life for them through plays. The Catholic Church was powerful enough to help put a stop to the traveling entertainers, whom they viewed as sinful. They stepped in as patrons and started funding entertainers to perform more Biblical types of entertainment. Plays and musicals with a religious theme were held originally in monasteries and churches, and later on outside of the church.

As the number of towns and art guilds grew, there were more and more opportunities for artists of all kinds. The church was still a big patron of the arts and would monitor the material that was presented, whether it was performed at a church or not. In essence they were censors, even when the production wasn't funded by them. Christmas and Easter festivals were popular during the Medieval times. Since church services were conducted in Latin, many people had a hard time understanding them. So the priests made a point of acting out the events, playing all of the parts, such as the three wise men and the Virgin Mary. Performances could be quite elaborate with candles, music, and the smell of incense burning throughout the church. As they grew more elaborate, they moved them out beyond the church into the courtyard, and ordinary people started playing the parts.

There were three types of plays at the time that reflected Christian principles. The first was the mystery play, which used priests and monks as the actors. The plays had four or five acts and were used to teach people about the Bible. Each act was performed at a different place in the town and usually ended right outside the church about the time the church services were to start to entice people to go in and listen to the day's sermon. It isn't known exactly why the mystery plays were called that, but it could be because the word mystery means "religious truth" or it could come from the word "misterium," which was the word for craftsmen.

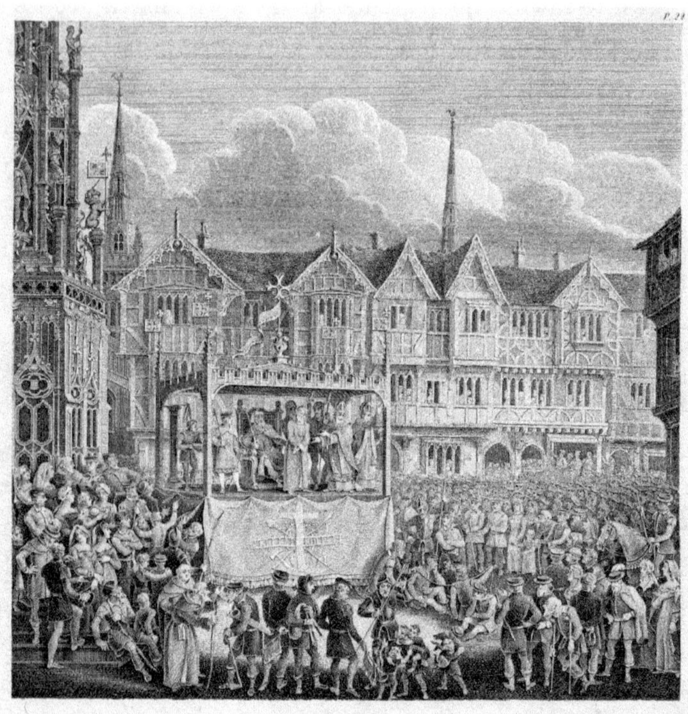

In England these mystery plays were performed on pageant wagons because there were no permanent theaters. Each one told a different story and would move from place to place around town. The top of the wagon was where the play was performed and the bottom part was where the actors changed costumes. They were similar to modern day parade floats. Each wagon was built by a different trade guild and the stories related to their particular guild. Examples include shipwrights performing Noah's Ark and the shepherd's guild performing the story of the nativity. The second type of play, the miracle play, revolved around the lives of saints. Quite often they were stories about the history of the miracles they had performed that made them saints. The most common stories featured the Virgin Mary, St. Nicolas, and St. George. It's rare to find any of these kinds of plays around today.

And the third type of play was the morality play, designed to teach a lesson on the right way to live according to the church. But instead of being a typical Bible lesson, the morality plays were focused on the common man. In fact, one of the most well-known of these is called "Everyman." The theme of every morality play had to do with the struggle for salvation and saving a soul. It was the classic story of good vs. evil, which is still a popular theme in today's media. A lot of symbolism was used in these types of plays, and they were usually serious but could also include some humor.

In the Renaissance, it was Pope Nicholas V who kicked off the surge of papal patronage just as the humanist movement was gaining traction. He became known as "the Humanist" because of all the resources he devoted to learning. He founded the Vatican library and invested heavily in the translation of Greek literature. Pope Nicholas V also sponsored numerous architectural and art projects in Rome. His wish was to turn Rome into a huge literary and artistic hub, and he encouraged artists to create there by supporting them financially and spiritually.

The papacy played a very important part in the art explosion of the Renaissance. Nicholas was not the only patron Pope. Others as well commissioned some of the best artists of that time and collected large amounts of art. Pope Sixtus IV commissioned some of the greatest painters of the day to paint the walls of the Sistine Chapel, the papal chapel that bears his name. One of these artists was Sandro Botticelli who contributed to the chapel walls the "Events of the Life of Moses," "The Punishment of Korah," and "The Temptation of Christ." Though when most people think of the Sistine Chapel they only think of Michelangelo, Botticelli and other artists such as Cosimo Rosselli had been commissioned to paint the chapel a good thirty years earlier.

Another Pope well known for his art patronage was the powerful and very ambitious ruler Pope Julius II. His papacy coincided with the High Renaissance, a time when art flourished. He was an art patron before he even became Pope. His goal was to return Rome to its original Golden Age and to bring fame to himself. His huge art collection was paid for by the sale of indulgences, a practice where the church would take a donation in exchange for one's soul going to heaven more quickly, therefore reducing time spent in purgatory.

He commissioned the reconstruction of St. Peter's Basilica and the painting of the Sistine Chapel by Michelangelo. The relationship between Pope Julius and Michelangelo was a rocky one from the start. Michelangelo originally was reluctant to take on the job because he felt that he was more of a sculptor than a painter, and he also had a disagreement with Julius about the way the painting was to look. Eventually Julius agreed to let him paint it the way he wanted and Michelangelo took on the job eventually firing all of his assistants and taking on the whole project himself. Julius complained constantly about how long it was taking to paint (over four years), and Michelangelo complained about how long it was taking to get paid.

Julius was followed by Pope Leo X, or Giovanni di Lorenzo de Medici, who was crowned Pope at the tender age of 37. He was a great patron of the arts and culture. Writers, musicians and artists traveled to Rome to win his patronage, and those who were qualified were offered positions in the church. As soon as Giovanni was crowned, he started spending huge amounts of money on his passion for the arts, which eventually needed to be paid for by the sale of indulgences. Like his father, Lorenzo the Magnificent, Pope Leo was a connoisseur of the arts who enjoyed poetry, fine art, and music. Artists were paid high salaries under his rich patronage, and musicians played on the best instruments money could buy.

One of those artists was Raphael, who found patronage in both Julius II and Leo X. He was commissioned to decorate the Vatican Stanze and painted ten tapestries to be hung in the Sistine Chapel. He also received patronage from wealthy bankers. One of his patrons was the Sienese banker, and banker to the Pope, Agostino Chigi. He owned an elaborate villa next to the Vatican where he held lavish parties to show off his enormous wealth. Raphael's many patrons made him rich and famous.

Pope Leo expanded Rome's position as the center of the literary world. He collected as many manuscripts and books as he could find. He lavished gifts, money favors, and jobs on actors, poets, and playwrights, often commissioning them to write and perform plays. Martin Luther, the German monk and theology professor, was greatly troubled by this belief that your ticket to heaven was for sale through the purchase of indulgences. But many in the Catholic Church felt that doing good deeds, like commissioning artworks for the church, was a way to get into heaven. They felt that through doing good, people had some hope of salvation in their lives.

⁂

Another type of performer prominent in Medieval times was the minstrel. If a minstrel didn't get patronage from the king, they spent their lives traveling from town to town, castle to castle, usually on a mule, collecting donations from appreciative audiences along the way. Minstrels dressed in colorful costumes and played an instrument like the harp. In keeping with the religious Christian themes of the times, minstrels sang songs about the Bible, the miracles of saints, and legendary Christian warriors. Sometimes the best ones would be swooped up by kings, bishops, or princes to work for them full-time.

Normally one might not connect great music with the Middle

Ages, but it was actually a period of great musical achievement and this rebirth started even before the Renaissance. Music seemed to be everywhere, especially in the late Middle Ages when many talented composers seemed to come out of the woodwork.

Pope Gregory I, known as the "father of Christian worship" during the Middle Ages, is also the patron saint of singers and musicians. The Gregorian chant, a monophonic series of chants or plainsong used in the Western Church, is named after him. This type of music was revived in the 1950s and again in the 1980s with bands like Enigma; their haunting Gregorian Chant "Sadeness" became an international hit. Another German band named Gregorian performs modern pop and rock songs with a Gregorian chant backdrop.

Hymns and psalms were popular in the Middle Ages and were often played on stringed instruments such as the harp or lyre. Now Christian artists are reviving old hymns and giving them a more modern twist. Keith and Kristyn Getty have carved out a niche for themselves as modern hymn writers. They've taken their love for the traditional hymn and turned it into a publishing and performing empire. According to their website, *Getty Music.com*, their hymn "In Christ Alone" has been the most frequently sung hymn in UK churches for the past nine years. According to *CCLI*, an estimated 40 to 50 million people sing it in church services each year, which does not include its popularity throughout Asia. Many modern hymnbooks now list the Getty as their most featured composers and their hymns are used increasingly both in contemporary and traditional circles.

Art in the Middle Ages was created to glorify God, not for self-expression, but the "re-birth" of the Renaissance meant the emergence of humanism. Renaissance humanism was believed to have started with the Italian poet Francesco Petrarch who is often called "the father of humanism" or even the "father of the Renaissance." Petrarch was a devout Catholic and believed that God gave humans intelligence and creativity that were intended to be used to the fullest. He didn't see a conflict between his faith and his secular achievements. In fact, if anything, he felt they complimented each other.

Early humanists, like Petrarch, studied the poets of Ancient Rome such as Cicero and Virgil, and realized there was a better, more effortless style of life—an inspiring life that included poetry, science, philosophy, and art. Painters, such as Giotto di Bondone, and writers like Dante Alighieri, used the humanist style to change the way art was created. Petrarch's goal was to awaken in the people of Italy a new sense of rebirth and consciousness, and indeed the Renaissance became a period where people had a renewed sense of classical learning, values, and the beauty of art.

During the humanist movement, people started to look inward and question themselves and everything around them. Like Petrarch, Renaissance humanists were often devout Christians who also promoted secular values. Petrarch's patron was the church. He was a cleric and traveled as a diplomatic envoy. This allowed him the time and funds to write poetry, sonnets, and letters, and also to pursue his passion—searching for forgotten classical texts. He accumulated quite an impressive collection by the later part of his life. These texts would come in handy for him when the plague spread through Europe as he could escape to Venice and exchange them for a house.

The church continued to be a big patron of the arts, but as the Renaissance took hold and humanism became popular, their patronage extended to cover the public and private sectors as well as the religious. Religion didn't vanish but became a more subtle part of music, literature, sculpture, and artwork. Secular and human interests became more prominent. Curiosity and individual freedom of expression challenged authority and the strict dogma of the church. Artists were no longer constrained to getting their patronage solely from the church, as they were in the Middle Ages, but were also free to pursue secular patronage. Religious art continued throughout the Renaissance, but it was often commissioned by wealthy nobles and merchants.

⤚

Today you rarely see church patronage. Much of that role has been replaced by museums and non-profits. But an organization called By/For is looking to change that. They hope that churches will reclaim their role as patrons of the arts and support Christian artists. In turn, church patronage will strengthen their communities. By/For projects are licensed under Creative Commons and allow churches to use the art for the good of the community. In this way, the internet has changed art—so many more people are able to enjoy it.

While art in the Middle Ages was almost exclusively Christian or religious, Christian art today is a much smaller market. But there are artists who are making sure that market still exists, like a group of artists called Jesus Painter Ministries. As it says on their website, *Jesus Painter.com,* "We bring faith to life in living color through live painting performances, artistic workshops and training the next generation of artists." They perform live art during church sermons, conferences and retreats.

There is also a subset of artists called Christian speed painters, like color-blind painter Lance Brown. It's impressive enough that he paints excellent pictures of Jesus in five minutes, but he can also do it upside down. Lance performs his art for conferences, fundraisers, private parties and weddings. Sue Falcone is a writer with a book in the Christian market called *The Lighthouse of Hope* that chronicles her own journey from fear to a stress-free life. Being the entrepreneurial artist that she is, she self-published the book and now sells it online. Realizing there was a need for Christian writers to have more information about the business side, she started her own Christian Writers Conference. On top of that she also runs a speaker bureau called "Remarkable Speakers" and constantly touts the benefits of the entrepreneurial lifestyle for all artists and speakers.

Times have changed for the modern Christian artist, but Brett McCracken, author of *Hipster Christianity: When Church and Cool Collide,* probably would have fit right in at a seminar of humanist Renaissance writers. Like Petrarch, he is on a quest to discover what it means to be Christian and cool. How can you be a Christian and still immerse yourself in pop culture? Hipster churches are popping up everywhere, and a new wave of alternative Christian singers, writers, musicians, speakers, and filmmakers are making a name for themselves in this new and burgeoning market.

Alternative Christian rock started taking off in the 80s and has been gaining in popularity ever since. Christian pop artists include Francesca Battistelli, Adrey Assad, Avalon, and Jars of Clay. Christian rock groups like Casting Crowns, Litehouse, and Stryper are among some of the more popular groups. There are Christian metal bands like The Devil Wears Prada, Demon Hunter, Red, and Oh Sleeper and punk rock Christian bands like I am Empire and Relient K. And there are even Christian rap and hip hop groups like Tedashii and Tobymac.

Christian music groups can get sponsorship through churches and corporations. Pepsi sponsored Christian musicians and featured them on special limited edition cans of their most popular sodas. Each can included a link to get a free download from several Christian artists. The Winter Jam Tour Spectacular is a large and very popular Christian music tour sponsored by Pepsi, local Christian college University of Mobile, The OverFlow.com, and other churches, non-profits, and corporations.

⁂

The first Christian or faith-based films weren't really films but slides projected on the wall using something called a magic lantern. These primitive slide projectors, which used a candle or a lamp, were popularized by Catholic priest Athanasius Kircher in 1680. In the 1800s missionaries used them to spread the gospel in Africa.

A 1911 pamphlet written in Exhibitors' Times by Herbert A. Jump called "The Religious Possibilities of the Motion Picture" talked about film being the most important invention since the printing press. Jump wrote "The visible drama shown in the right sort of motion picture, accordingly, has religious possibilities just as the spoken dramatic story or parable has them. Both help to make the Gospel vivid."[9]

Many faith-based films have hit the box office over the years, including Cecil B. Demille's 1956 epic *The Ten Commandments*, which was nominated for seven Academy Awards including Best Picture. It was one of the most financially successful films ever made, grossing over $122 million during its initial release. Few faith-based films would enjoy that level of success until Mel Gibson's *Passion of the Christ* in 2004. It was turned down by every major studio, so Gibson's own production company made it for $30 million and it grossed over $600 million internationally, making it one of the top grossing films in history.

Many faith-based films are character-driven and can be shot in a limited number of locations to keep the costs down. This was the case with *God's Not Dead*, a film starring Kevin Sorbo as an atheist college professor who forces his students to write "God is Dead" on a piece of paper as an assignment. But one student refuses to do it and debates his professor on the topic. The film was made on a $2 million budget and grossed over $62 million.

The Christian market for artists of all kinds continues to grow. Christian artists who choose to be entrepreneurial and chart their own path can find sponsors who want to align themselves with that message.

---

9 Herbert A. Jump, Exhibitors. Volume 1 "*The Religious Possibilities of the Motion Picture*," 15.

Open a Bank Account and Get a Free Monogrammed Chalice

How banks revolutionized the art industry

"Money never declines. Money just moves."

Dick Kovacevich,
former chairman and CEO of Wells Fargo

Because of Italy's geographical location, its cities became trading posts connecting Europe to the Byzantine Empire. Venice, Florence, Rome, and Milan became wealthy and powerful cities and the cradle of capitalism. The economy went from feudal to capital based. Before the Renaissance, artists were mostly anonymous craftsmen. If you didn't work for either the church or for royalty there's a good chance you were a starving artist. And you certainly weren't able to paint or sculpt anything you wanted and make money from it like you can today. But there's one industry that would change that for all artists… banking.

Before the Renaissance, it was strictly forbidden by the Roman Catholic Church for Christians to charge interest (usury) for loaning out money. It was considered to be taking advantage of the poor. But the Medicis, an innovative banking family, found ways around that. They did it by lending in one currency but collecting in another. Also they would sometimes lend money to merchants in exchange for price discounts.

The powerful Medici dynasty all started with a humble man named Giovanni di Bicci de' Medici, who would kickstart a reign over Florentine politics and culture that would last for almost 300 years. He started out as an apprentice to his cousin, who owned a chain of banks and taught Giovanni everything he knew about banking. Once Giovanni decided to strike out on his own his timing was perfect. Even though he didn't have much money he had a couple of things on his side. One was his friendship with the Pope. The other was the incredible economy that was booming thanks to trade flowing from Florence.

Giovanni's bank, The Medici Bank, was expanding into other branches. But the business really took off when his friend the Pope decided to open an account there. Networking was the key to success in those days, and you didn't get any bigger than the Pope. Within a few years, the Medici Bank grew into one of the most successful businesses in all of Europe.

The Medicis were banking innovators. One of the things they did was to have multiple branches of the bank in different cities that were run by branch managers, who also received a generous share of the profits. Giovanni's networking also paid off in other ways. He was rewarded with tax-farming contracts and the rights to many valuable alum mines, pretty much giving them a monopoly on alum. Alum was used to purify drinking water in those days, along with other uses, such as in the textile industry.

But Giovanni, who was known as a just and virtuous man, felt that he should be giving back some of the "ill-gotten gains." One rule of the church stated that only full restitution of ill-gotten gains could insure that you got a ticket into heaven. Those ill-gotten gains had to be restored to their owner. Distribution of charity, in the church's eyes, wasn't enough. So, the Medicis, wanting to hedge their bets against eternal damnation, used their creativity to get around this as they had gotten around the usury law to charge interest. The way they cleansed their wealth and saved their souls was through art patronage. Even though they were giving their money away by sponsoring artists and donating this art to the public, they were clever in the way that they did it.

Giovanni was the first Medici in the family, but certainly not the last, to become a patron of the arts. He not only had a passion for it but felt it was his duty since artists needed wealthy patrons to sponsor them. They didn't do it just out of the goodness of their hearts. The art they commissioned served as a propaganda machine for the Medici dynasty.

But it was his son Cosimo who really accelerated their patronage and elevated their status in society. Cosimo spent lavishly on art commissioned from local painters, sculptors, and architects. Cosimo wanted to make sure the Medici name would live on forever. He knew that expensive works of art and buildings would keep the family name alive. He poured money into the building of churches, convents, colleges, and charitable institutions. Cosimo took over the Medici Bank after his father's death and turned it into a dynasty that held enormous power in Florence for centuries. He also commissioned the first public library at the monastery of San Marco in Florence. His wealth had a significant impact on Florentine society through his sponsorship of painting, sculpture, and architecture. He took a variety of artists and humanists under his wing, who all had different styles of art.

Even though Cosimo was one of the wealthiest men in Europe, he lived quite simply and saved his extravagant spending for his patronage. And though he spent time with other wealthy elite of Florence, he also spent time with the average citizens. This made him very popular among the public and helped create an image that was larger than life and made an impact on Florence. It also helped keep him in power as the lower classes held him in high regard.

Social networking during the Renaissance didn't quite mean the same as it does today. Clients sought out powerful patrons to build both their careers and their prestige. In this way networking through the patronage system was intrinsically linked to social climbing. Florentines understood how important patronage was to their careers and their livelihood. The process was very competitive. But if you could crack it, you received favors such as legal support, great jobs, marriage into the right families, tax forgiveness, and other benefits.[10]

Cosimo supported many artists and became known as a generous patron. Three of the artists he supported were Donatello di Niccolo di Betto Bardi, Fra Fillipo Lippi, and Michelozzo di Bartolommeo. Once Cosimo took control of the Florentine government, he had more power as a patron and commissioned those artists under the services of the Florentine government.

One of his first projects was meant to improve the city of Florence. He commissioned Michelozzo to create a magnificent palace for the Medici family. He realized that it couldn't be too opulent or the people wouldn't be in favor of it. But it was definitely a grand piece of architecture that reminded everyone who saw it how powerful the Medici family really was. Michelozzo also built the library of San Giovanni and Cosimo's summer villa at Careggi. Before Cosimo, artists were mostly anonymous. But Cosimo encouraged them to express their artistic talent and be individuals. He wanted them to get the credit and money they deserved.

One of the artists he encouraged was the sculptor Donatello. He was one of the greatest sculptors of 15th century Italy, before

---

10 For more on this see Paul D. McLean, *The Art of the Network: Strategic Interaction and Patronage in Renaissance Florence,* Durham, NC: Duke University Press, 2007.

Michelangelo's time. Donatello was an apprentice to well-known sculptors early in his career. He studied the very popular Gothic style, but he wanted a change from the old style and started creating his own. His masterpiece, David, was created in the old Gothic style but was innovative in that it was the first free-standing figure to be cast in bronze since classical times.

Donatello was also an innovator in his style, which was very lifelike and evoked strong emotions. He was known for making people and animals look very much like they do in real life. Cosimo and Donatello both shared a fascination with the ancient world, and they soon became close friends. Cosimo defended Donatello's homosexuality, even though it was against the law in Florence. Cosimo felt a paternal instinct towards Donatello, and he made sure he never lacked for work or money. He either paid Donatello himself to create a piece for him or he would recommend him to his wealthy friends.

Though he always had plenty of money, material wealth was not important to the eccentric artist. He was known to be very generous with his friends and even kept a basket full of cash suspended by a rope from the ceiling by the door. His friends and assistants were welcome to take whatever they needed without having to ask for it. Donatello never had a problem with Cosimo as a patron, but he was known to be moody with others. One merchant complained to him that a commissioned bronze head was too expensive, after Donatello had already completed it. The merchant wouldn't back down on the price, so Donatello smashed the piece in the street. The shocked merchant offered him twice the amount to redo it, but Donatello walked away. When Donatello was too old to work, he was given a farm to live on, which was close to the Medici estates.

Another eccentric "artiste" Cosimo supported was the painter Filippo Lippi. He was allowed to live in the Medici Palace while he worked on commissioned paintings for his generous and patient sponsor. Lippi had a problem focusing on his work and would often be late in finishing it. He was also known to slip out of the Palace, get drunk, and chase women when he was supposed to be working on a commissioned piece of artwork. Cosimo even resorted to locking him in the palace, but Lippi tied some bedsheets together and lowered himself out of the window. Cosimo finally unlocked the door and decided to let him come and go as he pleased, as long as his work got done. After that, Cosimo would tell other patrons that artists should be treated with respect.

The Medicis weren't the only bankers in Florence at the time. Tomosso Spinelli was a wealthy silk and wool merchant who was also a banker almost on the level with the Medicis. He chose to work his way up in society through business instead of through politics. And like other bankers of that time, he became a staunch patron of the arts, leaving his mark on society through the sponsorship of art and architecture. He donated generously to the church of Santa Croce and commissioned palaces and villas that bore his family's name.

Another banking dynasty was the Peruzzi family. They were one of the leading banking families before the Medici. They too established themselves as art patrons in Florence. Giovanni Peruzzi commissioned the painter Giotto to paint the chapel walls of the Basilica of Santa Croce with fresco murals honoring John the Baptist and John the Evangelist. Through a series of bad loans and massive debt, the Peruzzis declared bankruptcy, which contributed to the economic depression of the late Middle Ages.

The other major "super bank" of the time was the Bardi family. Like the Peruzzis, they loaned money to Edward the III of England during the Hundred Years War. Edward defaulted on his loans and was partially responsible for causing both families to go bankrupt. The Bardis and the Peruzzis were known as the "Rothschilds of the Middle Ages." The Bardis were also successful merchants and continued on after the bankruptcy. They were also known as patrons to the friars.

This combination of expanding trade in Italy, the rise of the middle class, and the proliferation of art patronage among the merchants, suddenly added more people to the role of art patron. Art and business were constantly intertwined. Banks loaned money to merchants. Merchants had more money to spend and needed artists to help their businesses. More people had money to spend on entertainment, and artists became entrepreneurs in their own right. The Renaissance was a great time to be a small business owner or an artist.

Artists were known for their art for the first time in history. They signed their paintings and became "brand" names. Small business merchants wanted to follow in the footsteps of the wealthy nobles and become creators themselves. Everyone was able to support the arts as a patron in some way, just like the crowdfunding craze is doing now. As small business merchants moved up financially, they started giving gifts of art to churches, hospitals, and libraries. They sponsored music and the theater. And the public attended performances put on by artists and merchants. Surprisingly, this collaboration between small business and artists has never reoccurred in history on such a big scale since the Renaissance.

∾

The sponsorship of artists by banks continues to be strong. In fact, according to research conducted by IEG, banks are still nearly twenty times more likely than other sponsors to put their support in the arts. In the 60s, Chase Manhattan Bank president David Rockefeller put together one of the first corporate art collections for both clients and employees to enjoy. Since then other banks have bought artwork that they displayed in their offices and lobbies.

The David Rockefeller Fund, along with J.P. Morgan Chase, Deutsche Bank, New York Yankees Foundation, and Change for Kids, Inc. all sponsor the School Partnerships and Education Program. Their Group Visits Program is a service to schools and community groups put on by the Bronx Museum. The purpose is to foster visual literacy and critical thinking, which introduces school children to the basic elements of the artistic process.

Deutsch Bank owns the world's largest corporate art collection and has shown its support for arts education around the world. They have partnered with the Museum of Contemporary Art in Australia, where high school students and teachers from more than 1500 institutions have taken part in their educational art programs. Deutsch Bank sees their investment in the community as a positive way to support artists, future artists, and art lovers.

U.S. Bank is a proud supporter of local arts organizations such as the Oregon Shakespeare Festival in Ashland, Oregon; The Fifth Ave. Theatre in Seattle, Washington; Playhouse in the Park in Cincinnati, Ohio; and Art on the Streets in Colorado Springs, Colorado. Chase Manhattan Bank is known for being a big sponsor of dance. They sponsored a national tour of the Dance Theater of Harlem. JP Morgan notes on their website that they view the arts as "the lifeblood of vibrant communities," and they support a wide range of events and programs that foster creativity and self-expression.

ING sponsors cultural projects around the world. Their goal is to make art both accessible to a broad audience and to support it at the local level. Bank of America believes culture "connects societies and economies throughout the world." They support numerous art programs, including Museums on Us, which grants cardholders access to over 150 museums around the U.S. and the Art Conservation Project, which preserves cultural treasures from around the world; they are also the global sponsor for the Chicago Symphony Orchestra.

Some banks have even started lending out complete, ready-made shows to art museums. These are basically turnkey exhibitions, and though a lot of museums may have balked at that in the past, now, in a down economy, they are embracing it. Many banks are starting to realize that they can launch an effective sponsorship campaign at a local level with smaller community museums, art exhibits, art councils, and individual artists. These sponsorships help to enhance their visibility, position them as a corporate leader, and improve their goodwill in the public's mind.

They've also realized that the sponsorship of art in general paints a great, philanthropic image in the minds of current and future clients, especially art lovers. Investment in a bank's community is simply a smart way to do business.

The Rise of the Dilettantes

"Youth, which is so soon over and gone
Let him who would be happy
Seize the moment
For tomorrow may never come"

Lorenzo di Medici

After living in the Middle Ages, where death, war and struggle often made for a bleak life, people hungered for something more uplifting. This came in the form of humanism. It was a new way of thinking that forced humankind to look inside themselves for introspective reflection. With the dawn of the humanist era, more and more amateur artists came out of the woodwork. These dilettantes were usually wealthy patrons of the art who wanted to dabble in the arts themselves, and they usually did so in many different kinds of art.

Many of them were noblemen who didn't need to make a living with art, and had more freedom to experiment solely on the projects they wanted to do. England's King James I was a patron of many artists, including Shakespeare, but he was also a dilettante writer himself. One of his books, *Daemonologie*, was a discussion of witchcraft, demons, ghosts, and fairies presented in Socratic dialogue.

Another one of Shakespeare's patrons was Queen Elizabeth. Like King James, she too was both a patron and a dilettante. Her musical ability was mostly known in certain privileged circles, as she mostly performed in private in her palace rooms. She was a singer, played the lute, and composed dance music but chose to keep her musical talent on the down low because female musicians and singers at the time were chastised for being frivolous and sexually loose. Yet noble women at the time were expected to have musical training and education so they could become top patrons of the arts. Elizabeth, like others, would need to have the correct knowledge in order to judge other artists when needed.

In the 16th and 17th centuries, 'the masque' was a festive courtly extravaganza that included singing, dancing, acting, and music. Costumes and set design were elaborate and were meant to be a tribute to the patron of the event. Acting and singing parts were filled by professional performers, and such royals as Henry VIII and Charles I, as well as Louis the XIV of France, all danced and performed in the masques at their court.

Members of the Italian courts often referred to themselves as dilettantes. They could indulge in the arts, mostly painting, poetry, and music, simply for entertainment, without pay. Just the title of dilettante put them in a higher social class. In France a dilettante was called an amateur. Being a professional in the arts at that time was considered scandalous and immoral. So, many men and women in the upper classes were actually prohibited from taking money for their creative efforts.

Humanists, such as poet and scholar Francesco Petrarch, studied ancient Roman poets such as Cicero and Virgil and realized there was a better, more effortless, style of life—an inspiring life that included poetry, science, philosophy, and art. So, for many the

Renaissance became a period where people had a renewed sense of classical learning, values, and the beauty of art.

Clearly, the key to social status during the Renaissance was through art patronage. For the upwardly mobile artist it was almost impossible to reach super star status without patronage. But patronage also benefited the patron. Sponsoring several artists and having an entourage follow you around town proved that you had wealth and status in the community. Until artists actually struck out on their own, it was well-known that the patron was considered the creator of the artwork.

So it wasn't a big jump for a patron to actually start believing that they could also be an artist. This is where the term dilettante came from: "A person with amateur interests in the arts." These days the word is more derogatory in its meaning and is used to describe someone who wants to be an artist but lacks the skills and the talent to actually make a living from it.

One of the most famous dilettantes and patrons of the Renaissance was Lorenzo di Medici, grandson of Cosimo di Medici and heir to the Medici banking fortune. Little Lorenzo didn't have a usual childhood. He was born into luxury and into one of the most powerful families in Italy. His father Piero groomed him to be a leader from a very early age. He was a precocious child with an air of confidence and sophistication that was unusual for someone of his age. This didn't go unnoticed by his father and grandfather. They saw an opportunity to prime him for a life of power, and prepare him to lead not only the family business but Florence as well.

When he was five years old they dressed him in the latest fashion and sent him to visit the Duke of Anjou. Lorenzo did not disappoint and carried on charming conversations fit for an adult. From that moment on, both father and grandfather knew they had a mini "star" in their midst. Lorenzo was constantly sent out to represent the Medici family. They nicknamed him "Lord of the Baths" and put him in charge of parties and picnics. Lorenzo was a natural born leader, and his family couldn't be happier. When he was a teenager his father sent him on diplomatic missions and trips to Rome to meet important political and religious figures like the Pope. He had an enormous amount of responsibility placed on him, and he often felt like he missed out on having a normal childhood.

He inherited his writing talent from his mother, Lucrezia Tornabuoni, who wrote sonnets and poetry. She was from a long line of nobles and was well-versed in culture. She made sure her children were also and hired tutors to teach them about politics, business, accounting, and philosophy. Lorenzo's teachers were diplomats, bishops, and humanist philosophers. Lorenzo enjoyed writing poetry when he was a teenager and was especially fascinated by sonnets, like his mother. Writing was his method of escape and relaxation, and he poured his personal inner struggles onto the page and was greatly influenced by Petrarch who believed that poets and artists were important members of society who could provide deep insight into the human soul. His grandfather Cosimo liked to make money with everything he learned. He felt that creating art of any kind was frivolous unless you made a profit with it. Lorenzo wasn't that way. He wrote poetry, not to make money from it but just for the sake of writing. He claimed it relaxed him.

Lorenzo was fortunate to be born into a family of wealth but was also fortunate to be born at a time when humanism and art were being reborn and intersecting each other. European scholars rediscovered Greek and Latin texts, and by the mid-15th century, humanism was taught as a curriculum, including poetry, philosophy, and rhetoric. Part of Lorenzo's education came from politicians, dignitaries, philosophers, and scholars who would drop by the Medici home and often stay for dinner. He picked up an enormous amount from the conversations he was exposed to. This was just a normal way of life for the family. It would have been a stimulating environment for anyone, and especially for a child of his age.

Lorenzo received the best schooling money could buy and

immersed himself in his humanist studies. He was a charming chameleon who could converse in Latin with scholars during the day over a glass of wine or hang out with laborers in the bars at night, trading bawdy tales and ale. In Florence, it wasn't unusual for the rich to mingle with the poor. The Medicis were known to mingle with everyone. Lorenzo would hang out with anyone who stimulated him spiritually and intellectually, even if they lived in a more sordid neighborhood. He liked being able to escape the formality of the palace and politics, and he did so as often as he could.

During the Renaissance, charity was an obligation and necessity for any family who wanted power and prestige. That was never a problem for Lorenzo, and he never turned away the poor. He was well aware of the distinct differences between his lavish upbringing and the struggle his neighbors endured. But having such a pedigree and power meant that he never really knew who his true friends were. If you were a "friend of Lorenzo" some of that power was transferred to you, and artists knew it. Young writers and artists would often latch onto him for that very reason, even if there was a genuine feeling behind it. It came as no surprise that Lorenzo would become known as one of the most prolific patrons of his time.

By the age of twenty Lorenzo mourned both the passing of his father Piero and his own youth. He wrote about it in his poetry and waxed nostalgic about the fact that he would now have to take over the family business and become a leader to his nation. With that came a great amount of responsibility. There were salaries of many employees to pay, upkeep on the huge estates and factories, and more money than he could ever spend in his lifetime. He had access to a world that most people, especially at his age, would never even know.

With his background and love for the arts, taking over as patron of the family was easy for Lorenzo. He had a deeper understanding of art, both from a technical perspective and aesthetically, than either his father or grandfather. He wanted to make sure the art patronage legacy of the Medici name would live on, and he wanted his own name to be linked with Florence art culture in perpetuity. Lorenzo continued to carry on the patronage his father and grandfather started and turned Florence into a leading center for art and literature.

He was always surrounded by artists, poets, and scholars. He found them to be more entertaining than the stuffy politicians he often had to spend time with. He liked to be around comedians and pranksters, who always lifted him out of the bad moods he sometimes found himself in. The Medici farm in Fiesole was more of a cultural gathering place and recreational resort than a farm, with artists like Michelangelo, Botticelli, and Leonardo di Vinci dropping by to hang out in the garden. The writers in Lorenzo's discussion group who hung out at Fiesole became known as the Platonic Academy. It had been first sponsored by Lorenzo's grandfather Cosimo. The academy translated Plato's works into Latin and celebrated Plato's birthday every November. It was disbanded soon after Lorenzo's death.

Lorenzo kept artists like Michelangelo on his payroll and used them to maintain the city's prestige abroad. He was on a mission to win the respect of the world through art, and his art patronage would go far in any court in Europe. He also had so much power and influence that no major art project would have been able to go through without his seal of approval. Lorenzo hired the best artists in Florence to work for him and encouraged competition among them. He wasn't stingy with them and didn't mind if they worked for other patrons. He just wanted all artists to be successful and make as much money as they could. Lorenzo also spent much on the purchase of books and manuscripts for the library. A lot of scholars back then didn't like the idea of printing from movable type, but Lorenzo embraced it.

Lorenzo was known to loan out his best artists to other countries if he needed something from them. Leonardo di Vince,

Michelangelo, and Botticelli became his personal ambassadors creating alliances throughout Italy. Lorenzo did his best to export the Florentine culture and bring notoriety to Florence and himself. Cosimo and Piero had spent years accumulating huge collections of art and ancient manuscripts. Artists, poets and scholars who frequented the Medici villas and palaces had access to them and could learn a lot from being exposed to different styles of art. Lorenzo expanded the collection to include some of the finest works in Europe. Instead of just Italian artists, he had works from Flemish painters, such as Hans Memling and Jan van Eyck.

Lorenzo even had artists live with him in the family palace. Michelangelo was one of them. At thirteen, Michelangelo was working as an apprentice to painter Domenico Ghirlandaio when Lorenzo asked Ghirlandaio if he could have two of his best students. Michelangelo was chosen to live in the Medici palace and be schooled along with his own children. He even gave his father a job there. Michelangelo was now exposed to the same rich culture as Lorenzo. He became immersed in art, poetry, science, and philosophy. As soon as the Medicis opened the humanist academy, he attended the school and came in daily contact with some of the greatest humanists and philosophers of the time.

Michelangelo took up sculpting at the school. While at home in the palace, Michelangelo was working on a piece when Lorenzo happened to walk by. The piece was flawless. In fact, too flawless. Lorenzo said that old people didn't have all of their teeth. They were always missing some. On hearing this, Michelangelo knocked out some of the statue's teeth. This greatly impressed Lorenzo and from then on he helped the boy even more to further his career as an artist. He recognized his abilities as a genius and wanted to support him in any way possible.

Another artist that Lorenzo sponsored was Alessandro Botticelli. He was born into a poor family and would not have achieved such fame and fortune had he not been under the patronage of Lorenzo di Medici. Botticelli also lived in the Medici palace and so was also exposed to Lorenzo's circle of scholars, artists, poets, and other intellectuals. This influence encouraged him to create a new and bold genre of art. The Medici circle of friends always kept Botticelli busy with work. "Adoration of the Magi" was commissioned by a tax collector named Guaspparre dal Lama because he wanted to impress the Medicis. "The Birth of Venus" was a wedding present for Lorenzo's cousin, Lorenzo de Pierfrancesco de Medici. It was so controversial that it remained hidden from the public for half a century.

Lorenzo was well known for putting on lavish masked balls, festivals, tournaments, pageants, horse races, carnivals, football games, mock battles, circuses, and parades at his own expense for the enjoyment of the people of Florence. He knew they were important from a political standpoint to attract people to the city. Artists traveled from far away to take part in them. Lorenzo kept them busy building floats, making armor, and sewing costumes. Verrochio, Botticelli, and Pollaiuolo were some of the artists who were showcased in the productions.

Some of the greatest writers, artists, and composers were called on for the Royal Entry of a ruler into a city. In the late Middle Ages these often merged with lavish festivities where artists like Leonardo di Vinci, Andrea del Sarto, and Rubens were hired to create temporary decorations. For some artists like Inigo Jones or Jacques Bellange, it was probably their only job. Artists were also hired to make up festival books. These were similar to a souvenir program, describing the order of events and the speeches given, and were beautifully illustrated and sometimes customized for certain patrons to distinguish them from the mass-produced ones. [11]

Carnival is one of the most celebrated holidays in Italy. It takes

---

11 R. Mulryne and Elizabeth Goldring, *Court Festivals of the European Renaissance: Art, Politics, and Performance,* London, UK: Routledge, 2002.

place before the Catholic Church's season of Lent and involves lots of food, wine, dancing, and singing. Carnival was probably a pagan festival started in ancient Greece. Carnival festivities became more extravagant under Lorenzo's rule. He would organize parades with floats called "tronfi," and each parade had its own Carnival songs, many of them written by Lorenzo based on his poetry. He dabbled in music, both composing it and performing it, writing and performing at his many festivals. Some of the songs were written by a composer Lorenzo hired named Heinrich Issac while he was staying at the Medici court. After the Medici dynasty fell, the Carnival never really regained its colorful and extravagant past. Also, many of the Carnival songs, along with some art treasures and musical instruments, disappeared.

Dilettantism changed over the years. In 17th and 18th century England, art patronage was less often a matter for the king and was slowly being taken over by the aristocracy who wanted to establish themselves as the ruling elite. As the bourgeoisie gained more economic power, dilettantism grew. Dilettantes not only became collectors and connoisseurs of art but also amateur artists themselves, such as musician and businessman Samuel Pepys and composer Barbara Srozzi, who performed in private settings. Wealthy noble amateurs, like Handel and Steffani, wrote much of the Baroque chamber music, and thanks to their patronage of other artists, many independent composers were able to make a living. Poet and playwright Johann Wolfgang Goethe believed that the dilettante and the artist needed each other. He believed they should form a partnership and that the dilettante's role is to use their experience and knowledge to bring the artist recognition.

The dilettantes often felt an obligation to raise the bar on whatever industry they were involved with, whether it was music, writing, painting, or poetry. If they paid the money, they felt they were the owner of the art and that it needed to be cultivated through their superior tastes. In 1734, The Society of the Dilettanti was formed. It started out as an exclusive gentlemen's club made up of noblemen and scholars who wanted to elevate classical art and architecture in society. They were collectors of antiquities that were later donated to museums.

There is a long list of Americans from the Revolutionary period who became famous for being dilettantes. Thomas Jefferson believed in the importance of acquiring historical artworks and artifacts in the formation of a new nation. He was a patron to artists like John Trumbull, who painted "The Declaration of Independence" along with other scenes of the Revolutionary War. He also collected artifacts from the Lewis and Clark expedition and from Native Americans.

But Thomas Jefferson would be considered a dilettante because he was not only a patron of the arts but also an accomplished artist himself. Not only did he write the draft of the Declaration of Independence, but he was a prolific letter writer and was known to have written poetry. Another artistic talent he had that most people don't know about was in music. He said "Music is the passion of my soul," and he had an extensive collection of books on the subject, especially books on the violin. He had a large music collection that contained volumes of hymns, psalms, anthems, and works by masters such as Vivaldi and Handel. He learned to play the violin himself as a teenager and owned several over his lifetime.

Benjamin Franklin was another founding father who was a dilettante. He was a self-taught writer who used the pseudonyms Silence Dogood and Richard Saunders. Silence Dogood was his alter ego as a middle-aged widow, and Richard Saunders was his alter ego as a slightly dull country boy who believed in hard work and living a simple life. As Saunders, he wrote Poor Richard's Almanac and sold over 10,000 copies of it a year for 26 years. Besides his political life, he was also a printer, inventor, and scientist.

Over time, the artist was evolving from being considered a lower-class slave to an aristocrat of culture as the relationship between artist and patron slowly developed. Today there are new kinds of dilettantes. And the very definition of dilettante has changed to now impart a more negative connotation as a dabbler in the arts who excels at none.

With the anonymity of the internet there are more and more frustrated "wanna-be" artists than ever who are quick to trash another artist while they themselves don't have the skills, talent, or perseverance to actually make a living as an artist. A true artist is less likely to snub a fellow artist but will offer good, constructive criticism. This happens in all areas of art, from writers to musicians, actors, singers, etc.

The wealthy dilettante of today may have made their money in another field and can afford the best equipment, coaches, and supplies money can buy, but that doesn't mean they will have what it takes to become a working artist. One thing that may be missing is the pure hunger, such as artists like Jewel or Steve Harvey had while they were living in their cars.

The original meaning of dilettante as someone who is both a lover and financial supporter of the arts as well as a dabbler who doesn't need to make a living from it is making a comeback. One example is from the Metropolitan Museum of Art. More than half of the security guards on staff are actually artists themselves. Since they are employed, technically they don't have to make a living from their art, but most of them want to. Many of these security guards actually have quite an impressive background in art education, including PhDs.

Another example would be the sheer number of bloggers who dabble in blog writing with no professional education and who don't need to make a living from all of their hard work. They do it because they enjoy it. There are also many speakers who have had a successful career or business and have now retired from the job or sold the company. They want to continue to work in some kind of creative capacity, so a lot of them will write books and turn to public speaking to occupy their time.

One example is Susan Packard. She was the co-founder of Scripps Networks Interactive and former chief operating officer of HGTV. Her new book *New Rules of the Game: 10 Strategies for Women in the Workplace* is about helping women navigate their way through the workplace using gamesmanship. She also speaks on the same topic.

Another example is Brian Smith, Founder of the iconic international brand UGG Boots. Brian wrote a book called *Birth of a Brand* and now travels around the world speaking to business owners about his entrepreneurial journey of how he started Ugg Boots in his garage and turned the brand into a multi-million dollar sensation.

My wish is to create many entrepreneurial artists around the world who will reach the stage of being a dilettante, then turn around and sponsor other up and coming artists to create a new generation of entrepreneurs.

Artists and the fans who love them

*"All the world's a stage, and all the men
and women merely players"*

William Shakespeare

The plays of William Shakespeare, one of the most prolific and successful writers in history, are the most read and performed in the world and have been translated into dozens of different languages. Shakespeare has become a cottage industry—his plays are performed in theaters around the world every night of the week, as he would have wished as they were intended to be enjoyed live instead of just read.

He is credited by the Oxford English Dictionary with inventing over 3000 words and phrases, many still used on a daily basis even though most people aren't aware of their origin. This is amazing considering his limited education and the fact that there weren't even any dictionaries back then for him to consult. So, the next time you use these words or phrases you can thank Shakespeare:

accommodation, reliance, assassination, birthplace, radiance, watchdog, courtship, misquote, schoolboy, leapfrog, zany, "a fool's paradise, "without rhyme or reason", and "into thin air."

It's ironic that the man who became known for his theatrical productions didn't have access to pubic theaters as a child. That's because they didn't exist at the time. Luckily, the schoolmasters in his small town of Stratford believed the best way to teach their students Latin was to have them read and perform ancient plays. This may have helped awaken young Shakespeare's passion for playwriting as may have the companies of actors who would go on tour putting on dramatic presentations in any town that would welcome them. They were sponsored by a wealthy nobleman, and the actors would wear their "employer's" uniform.

Shakespeare might have been inspired by these traveling spectacles. Though there were few formally written plays, these presentations would have included some kind of storytelling, along with dancing, singing, acrobatics, and juggling. They were usually staged in a public place, like an inn or marketplace. A few years later, James Burbage would build the first permanent theater dedicated to such companies, and one day it would put on most of Shakespeare's productions.

Shakespeare was born at a time when England had a strict class system, and he wasn't born into a family of wealth or nobility. He also didn't marry into wealth. But he probably inherited his most valuable trait, entrepreneurship, from his father. One of the reasons Shakespeare became so successful was because he was as much of a businessman as he was an artist.

There were several occurrences that created a perfect storm for Shakespeare. Both good and bad fortune shaped the way his career was formed. The first may have been when his father's business started going under. Young Shakespeare was yanked out of college because of lack of money. By the age of eighteen he had already gotten married and had his first kid. By the age of twenty-one he had three kids and a wife to support. Unlike his unemployed single artist friends, he was forced to earn a living. This may have pushed him into being an entrepreneurial artist. But unlike his friends, he would become a steadily working artist.

Being a working artist apparently made some people jealous, like the well-known playwright Robert Greene. Greene was one of the most popular writers in London just as Shakespeare's career was taking off. Greene, who was Cambridge educated, looked down on Shakespeare as a country bumpkin and didn't feel he belonged in the company of the other Cambridge educated playwrights. Greene called Shakespeare "an upstart crow," a jab at him being an amateur and a social climber. What was threatening to Greene and other successful writers at the time was that while they were out drinking and partying in the taverns, Shakespeare was hard at work. He had a family to support and had to focus on making money.

Shakespeare also heavily benefited from the effects of the Renaissance with its explosion of working artists. No longer was it necessary to work for the King or the church. An artist could work for anyone who had the money to pay them. And the economy was booming; Shakespeare used this to his advantage, racking up as many patrons, and different types of patrons, as he could find. London was at the heart of the cultural Renaissance, and its poets and dramatists were some of the most popular in the world. Shakespeare's innovative writing style would put him ahead of the pack and take London by storm.

The last occurrence that affected Shakespeare was the invention of printing. This completely changed the way people communicated and shared ideas. These ideas could be printed up quickly and shared on a wide scale. Add to that the deaths of Shakespeare's competition, Robert Greene and his fellow playwright Christopher Marlowe; both died just as Shakespeare's career was taking off, leaving him no competition. It was a fabulous time to be an artist and an even better time to be William Shakespeare.

The traveling actors had freedom to launch any kind of play they wanted, but this could be seen as dangerous to the state and to the church. Queen Elizabeth worried this free speech could get out of control, so she started granting a license to wealthy patrons to maintain the troupes and keep them out of trouble. In other words, the patrons would be responsible for their artists' behavior.

But it actually became a great way for the clever artist to insure they had a steady paycheck. Patronage made the difference between a working artist and a starving artist. This is when Shakespeare learned the value of patronage and how important it was to an artist. His business skills and strong patronage throughout his lifetime meant he had a lot of free time to write. He knew that the creative process doesn't happen overnight, and artists needed to make a living like everyone else. Without patronage, Shakespeare's works would never have come to fruition, would never have been so prolific, and certainly would never have achieved the level of success throughout history that they achieved.

His first patron came along at exactly the perfect time. It was 1592 and the Bubonic Plague was breaking out in London. Theaters were boarded up and were ordered closed until further notice. This caught artists by surprise who relied on the theater for their livelihood. This is when Shakespeare sought out the patronage of the Earl of Southampton, a very wealthy and spoiled young man who was dipping his toe into the patronage of artists, especially poets. Shakespeare was already known for his plays and admired by the Earl.

Shakespeare courted him as a patron, as did many others. He was willing to do whatever it took. After all, he still had a family to feed, and writing plays wasn't going to pay the bills as long as the plague was raging on. At the time homosexuality was a crime, but close male friendships were expected. Was there something more to their relationship? Perhaps we'll never know. But Shakespeare knew that the Earl was facing a huge fine if he didn't marry by a certain age, and he was prepared to do his part in helping to resolve that problem. He pledged his service to the Earl.

Shakespeare quickly learned that the person who paid the bills was in charge. Even though he was an entrepreneur, he was able to adapt to being a subservient employee if he had to. This would serve him well, as he was free during this time to spend his hours writing without having to worry about where the money would come from to pay his bills. And when the plague was over, he was further along than many of the other writers of the time, who had spent their time touring through the countryside for whatever money and free meals they could get.

Shakespeare reinvented himself during this time by writing and publishing two long poems, "Venus and Adonis" and "The Rape of Lucrece." Writing poetry stretched his creativity and writing skills and ultimately made him rich. He dedicated both poems to his patron Southampton, who gave his seal of approval.

It also improved his profile as a writer. His playwriting improved, and he was ready to hit the ground running as soon as the theaters reopened. It also taught him to become more prolific. Being unemployed was something he couldn't bear to think about. And he never was. Shakespeare put his entrepreneurial knowledge and the money he earned writing poetry to work in one of the smartest moves of his career. He learned the value of being a business owner when he became a shareholder (with seven other shareholders) in the acting company Lord Chamberlain's Men. They shared the profits and the debts that were incurred by the company.

This guaranteed Shakespeare a place to act and launch his new plays, plus he benefited financially from being a part owner in the company. This also cemented his professional stability for more than twenty years, something no other actor or playwright of that time could declare. All of this run of good luck happened because he was willing to try something new, which was to get a wealthy patron and diversify his writing talent by learning new skills. Another reason he was able to write without having to worry about making a living is that he took his play earnings and purchased real estate. He bought the second largest house in his hometown of Stratford and purchased other real estate near Stratford that would earn him income for years to come.

Shakespeare's first royal patron was Queen Elizabeth. She loved drama, especially the study of the ancient classical period, and Shakespeare would perform for her at her court. "A Midsummer Night's Dream" was probably one of the plays that was done as a private performance. During the Queen's forty-five-year reign, London went through a cultural awakening, and England prospered during the second half of her reign. Professional theaters were built in England for the first time and her love of theater gave birth to literary geniuses such as Shakespeare, Christopher Marlowe, and Ben Jonson through her generous patronage. It was one of the golden ages in English literature.

In Shakespeare's day, going to the theater was a different experience than it is today. The audience would eat, drink, and talk during the performance; they would stand up and move around. And if the actor's performance wasn't up to par, they would throw fruits and nuts on the stage. The wealthier patrons could sit in covered galleries., but if you couldn't afford a good seat, you could pay a penny and stand in the pit. These audience members were called "groundlings" or "penny-stinkards."

After the cycle of the plays ended, most actors went on the road as a traveling troupe in their pageant wagons. Since it wasn't safe to park them by the side of the road, they had to stay in inns. The inns were fashioned in a U-shape, so they would back their wagons up to the gate, and the people staying in the inns would either stand in the courtyard or look through their windows to see the show. Since actors were notorious for not having money, the inn owners would take the nuts off of their wagons to ensure they got paid. This is supposedly where the phrase "making your nut" came from.

One of Shakespeare's first plays was "The Comedy of Errors." It was such a success when it was performed at one of London's law schools that students rioted to get in to see it. This marked the beginning of Shakespeare's "fan club." Shakespeare's fans were part of a community that helped spread the word about his plays. He listened to what they had to say and incorporated their feedback into his future productions.

When King James I took over the throne, he became the new patron of the Lord Chamberlain's Men acting company. In addition to performing on their own, which was basically fan patronage, they also performed about a dozen times a year at the court. King James is most widely known for commissioning the King James' version of the Bible, which was transcribed from Latin to English so it could be read by more people.

With a portfolio of wealthy patrons and a rabid following of fans of his plays, Shakespeare was able to do something few of his fellow artists could do: He simply made a living with his art alone. He was able to continue writing at a time when the plague had the theaters closed down; he used his time wisely, writing poems and sonnets when he couldn't make money writing plays; and he was diversified in his art and in his financial portfolio.

Shakespeare never wrote propaganda. His plays weren't a thinly veiled way of getting his own message across. He was an intellectual who loved the idea of debate and ideas. His plays put one idea up against the other and showed both sides, letting the audience decide for themselves. At a time when other playwrights gave up ownership of their plays and were paid little for their writing, Shakespeare retained creative control and got a percentage of the production as a producer.

⤸

Today, artists can do the same thing as an entrepreneur, though most still choose the traditional route of waiting to be hired by someone. This guarantees they will always be under someone else's control, will never get the lion's share of the profits, and won't have creative control. Some A list celebrities have managed to negotiate these things, but the A list makes up only a tiny fraction of artists out there. Today there are playwrights who want to follow in Shakespeare's shoes and create a career as an entrepreneurial artist where they do get creative control and profit sharing. These entrepreneurial artists are using the same methods the Lord Chamberlain's Men used, and some are even creating new business models that would make Shakespeare proud.

A good example of an entrepreneurial artist who has always done things his own way is Tyler Perry. He started as a playwright who turned his own personal tragedies into comedies. His first play was called "I Know I've Been Changed." He saved every dollar he could and invested it in a local production. Unfortunately, the only people who came to the play were people he knew, and most seats were empty.

But he had such a strong belief in himself that he refused to give up. Six years later that same play was sold out and he had to move it to a larger theater to accommodate the audience. His play "Madea On The Run," based on his sassy grandma, would also sell out in theaters across the country. Perry knew his audience, even when others said it couldn't be done. He wrote for them and continued to write for them, and they responded with their loyalty. He eventually expanded his audience and has had both artistic and commercial success. He now runs his own studio, which isn't based in Hollywood but in Atlanta.

Another example, an experimental theater group in Chicago called the Neo-Futurists, was originally formed to put on one specific show. They were the first late-night theater production in Chicago. "Too Much Light Makes the Baby Go Blind" was an eight-person ensemble who performed thirty plays in sixty minutes, all involving audience participation.

The group caught on quickly and became wildly successful with a steady and growing group of fans who loved their work. Their original late-night show is still a hit, and they've since added a whole season of exciting and innovative shows. One of them is the production "Writing and Drinking," a show about alcohol and great literature, performed in a local tavern. This was also so successful that it's spun off a radio show and a brewery. They've since been commissioned to do work for hire and released their own CD. The group tours and teaches as an extra income stream, assuring that they, like Shakespeare, can make a living purely from their art.

Teaching your art can be more than just an extra income stream, as fine artist Leonardo Pereznieto found out. He was struggling to make a living as an artist despite having traveled the world with successful gallery showings. He started a You Tube channel to showcase his art to as many people as he could. But it only got as far as his friends and family. One day he decided to record himself drawing a picture in pencil. This proved to be more successful, so he kept doing it, adding narration and actually teaching the audience how to do what he was doing. Every time he uploaded another demonstration video he would improve on his technique, and he expanded his reach by using other social media like Facebook and Twitter. By 2013 he achieved total freedom as an artist when his You Tube earnings alone started paying all the bills. He has since been asked to lecture at art schools around the world and is currently working on a book about drawing.

The Gorilla Tango Theater is different from most live theater companies, who are non-profit, and they approach it from the point of view of making the art the center of attention. Gorilla Tango approaches it as a for profit money-making venture first but also puts out good product. The founder, Dan Abbate, started out in the business world before taking on the challenge of running a theater. His background in manufacturing and technology gave him a unique advantage as far as marketing and sales are concerned.

Whether you're selling cars or peanuts or live theater, the bottom line is always… the bottom line.

Their producing deal is turnkey and doesn't require money up front from the producing companies. Profit is split 50/50 and 80 percent of the productions make money. The most successful shows have an opportunity to have extended runs and can be picked up for national distribution through Gorilla Tango Capital. Like the Neo-Futurists, Gorilla Tango Theater makes money teaching classes and is also working on distributing some of their more successful shows to theaters across the country. And, like many theaters, they also rent out their theater space by the hour for rehearsals.

Singer, songwriter, producer Jon Bellion also learned how to build up a fan base and turn it into a successful career. He instinctively knew that he needed to get the fan base first to increase his chances with touring and radio play, so he gave away his first few albums for free to gain traction. Even though he wasn't getting paid for it, he knew the material still had to be good. Once he transitioned to having his audience pay for albums he knew the material had to be even better. By the third headlining tour, 80 percent of the tour was sold out before the album came out. Another clever thing Bellion did for his fans was to produce behind the scenes videos. Where some artists would worry about showing all of the mystery behind the music, Bellion says it has only helped. Fans see all of the hard work that goes into the making of the album and they respect that. And Bellion lets his fans see the whole process, not just a teaser video.

For an entrepreneurial artist who is looking to build their fan base they need to give the fans something special they can't get anywhere else. They need to be able to have access to an artist from the beginning, by seeing them live on tour, through social media, podcasts, newsletters, or an interactive forum. They need to create unique content people will want to share with their friends and through social media.

With your own art, involve your fans in your artistic journey and take them along for the ride. Let them get to know you, why you became an artist, your background, and your personal story. People follow and buy from people they know and like. Build trust with them. Use their instantaneous feedback to improve your work and give them more of what they want to see of your art.

Fans will gravitate towards an artist, not just because of their talent, but also because of their own personality, as UK rock musician Rob Chapman found out. He was one of many struggling musicians trying to find his place in the industry, cobbling together day jobs and freelance gigs, writing jingles and teaching guitar lessons, when he stumbled on a formula that worked. In 2006 he placed a small guitar instructional video on My Space, and after two days he had gotten fifty views on it. Granted, that fifty views wasn't enough to change his life or his bank account, but it did prove to him that there is a much bigger world out there than he imagined who might be interested in buying what he had to sell. And what he had to sell, he realized, was more than just an instructional video.

In the beginning, he approached the videos as simply straight forward lessons on learning how to play the guitar. But over time he started to get a little looser with his delivery and let more of his inner rock star shine through. He was suddenly getting way more views that way and had come to the realization that getting fans was more about a brand than just conveying information.

Like all successful entrepreneurial artists find out, you eventually need to have multiple streams of income to stay ahead. Chapman found out that the fan base he had built up was valuable, and sponsors started calling him to do online reviews for their products. That was in addition to his income from You Tube ad dollars. He now does demos for a local UK retailer and has become a partner in a guitar manufacturing company. The company polls Chapman's followers about what they want in a guitar and sells them direct to retailers based on the feedback. But it doesn't even end there. Like Jon Bellion, thanks to his massive fan base, tour DVD pre-orders for his band Dorje made the tour instantly profitable. So, basically Chapman became the rock star he always wanted to be. He just took the entrepreneurial way through the backdoor to get there and has done it on his own terms maintaining creative control over his career.

Dancers and choreographers are also finding out that they can make a living as a You Tube star. Meghan Sanett is well known on You Tube as a choreographer, teacher, and dancer. She has millions of views on You Tube and is able to solely make a living doing what she loves to do. Tap dancer Jack Evans has performed for "Britain's Got Talent" and toured the world. His innovative style is also a big hit on You Tube, where he's expanding his brand beyond his native U.K.

Fans are critical to success, and one of the biggest and most famous group of followers were the Dead Heads, the name given to fans of the rock band The Grateful Dead. Dead Heads were fanatical about the band and literally followed them to as many concerts as possible. Since no two shows were ever the same, fans wanted to see them all. They even taped them with lead singer Jerry Garcia's blessing. Not only was he okay with fans taping their concerts, the band actually set up a taper's section. Fans would exchange tapes with each other since all of the performances were different. No money ever changed hands for the tapes and doing so was frowned upon.

Their fans were entrepreneurial, and they needed to be if they were going to pay to travel around following the band as a Dead Head. Many would sell food and T-shirts in the parking lot, and would then camp out in their multi-colored VW vans that they lived out of for months. There were Dead Head newsletters and magazines, and a lot of this historical material is now stored at the Grateful Dead Archive at UC-Santa Cruz.

Lady Gaga has a pet name for her followers too. They are known as Little Monsters. Her second album revolves around the monster theme. She developed the moniker of Mother Monster and started referring to her fans as Little Monsters. They now have their own symbol—a hand claw. When they agree with something she says, they do a "paws up." Just like the Dead Heads have their own language, Little Monsters use terms like Monsterlove or Monsterkisses among each other.

The bottom line is that people want to feel like they belong, like they are in a community of like-minded people. They want to contribute to that community, whether it's content, sharing of other people's content, or spending money. This is especially important if you decide to crowdfund.

I think the Bard would be fascinated to see the number of fan clubs, forums, book clubs, meet up groups, Twitter followers, and Facebook fans he has around the world today. Being the forward-thinking entrepreneur that he was, I think he would have been the first to embrace a form of communication that would allow him to reach so many new fans of his work. In his time, the closet thing they had to social media was either word of mouth or the playbill, handed out around town on the day of the play like the playbills of today, giving information about the play and the players.

For today's artists, fan engagement is critical, both online and off. Whether you're an actor, writer, speaker, filmmaker, musician, or any other type of artist, if you're good, you'll have fans. And those fans want to hear what you have to say. One way to keep in touch with them is through a blog or email newsletter. Give them timely information on what you're doing and where you'll be performing. What is your next project and where will it be seen?

Fans want to be able to say that they helped to participate in your success. This is one reason crowdfunding is so popular. They want to buy your CDs, books, and films because they know it keeps you in business. It enables you to keep creating more of what they want to see and hear. Learn as much as you can about your fans and find out what they like. Invite them to share comments on your blog. Send them a survey and ask them to give you feedback. You'll be surprised at what you get. This will not only help you improve as an artist but will help you to customize your material to the people who are your biggest fans. Do this online and off.

Get your fans to give you their email by giving them something in return, like a free unreleased single that they can't get anywhere else, a sneak peek at the trailer for your latest movie before anyone else sees it, free access to a music video or a video of a live performance, a chapter from your book, or some other freebie your audience would give up their email address for. Give your fans access to a private section on your website where you have your bio, pictures, special videos, publicity, behind the scenes clips, and anything else they would be interested in seeing. People buy from people they know, like and trust. Get them to know you, like you and trust you by letting them into your life.

How smart artists profit from their intellectual property

"What you are, you are by accident or birth; what I am, I am by myself. There are and will be a thousand princes; there is only one Beethoven."

Ludwig van Beethoven

One of the most prolific and innovative musicians and composers of the music world was Ludwig van Beethoven. Like many creative geniuses, his talent was a combination of his genes, upbringing, the social issues at the time, and his complete focus and dedication to his artistic ability. He came from a family of musicians, including his father Johann and his grandfather Ludwig, who were both government musicians.

Being poor meant his family didn't have the money for proper schooling and musical training, but his father, a moderately talented musician and music teacher, trained him as best he could. He was determined that his son Ludwig would become a household name in the music world, even if it meant whipping him to get him to practice. He would often stumble in late after a night of drinking at the pub, and drag young Ludwig to the piano and make him play until dawn. Beethoven was forced to give his first concert at the tender age of seven, though he resented being forced to perform for the public on cue.

As Johann's income dwindled, he saw his son as a potential breadwinner, or at least an extra source of income for the family. He trained him in the traditional style to prepare him to get a job as a court musician. By the time he was ten, his talent had attracted the attention of the ruler of his hometown of Bonn, Germany, where Ludwig was given the opportunity to study with the court organist, Christian Gottlob Neefe. Neefe immediately recognized the child prodigy's talent and nurtured it. By the time Ludwig was twelve he was put in charge of directing the court orchestra.

By this time Beethoven's genius was starting to show. One thing that made Beethoven unique was his ability to improvise. And it's the one thing his father tried to stifle in him early on. But being the stubborn and rebellious child that he was, he simply ignored it and continued to improvise for the rest of his life. It was his improvisational skills that would make him stand out from other musicians. He was always overly confident and self-sufficient. He realized he was gifted and flaunted it wherever he went. You could say he was one of the first real divas in the music industry, before the word was even used.

One of Beethoven's early piano students introduced him to the elite of Bonn society, where he was included in intellectual conversations about the latest ideas and events that were going on in Europe. He realized that he needed to leave Bonn for bigger opportunities in Vienna, which was becoming a hub of culture, music, and expanding wealth. Just like in Florence, Italy, there was a growing middle class of merchants in Vienna. They, along with the nobility, all needed and wanted to hire musicians and other artists, and there was plenty of money to go around.

This era came to be known as the Enlightenment. Beethoven was greatly influenced by the era, where the natural rights of man and the individual's role in society started to take center stage. It was a time of great innovation when people began to recognize their ability to think for themselves and create their own surroundings.

Beethoven was inspired by this new way of thinking, and it was reflected in his music. He wanted to write music that touched people emotionally and bridged the gap between the elite and the common man. He always believed that great music could and should benefit all of mankind. Though he wasn't terribly concerned about money, he knew if he wanted to eat he would have to have wealthy patrons paying him. But he never stooped to the level of a servant, as many musicians and artists were thought of during that time. He knew he was a genius, and he had tremendous confidence in his abilities.

His first patron upon arriving in Vienna was Prince Karl Lichnowsky. He was one of the wealthiest and most sought after patrons in Vienna. Beethoven was given a small apartment in the attic and a yearly salary. His arrogance and aloofness didn't turn off the elite, but instead gave Beethoven an air of eccentricity that they hadn't seen before. He developed many fans in the upper-class aristocratic circles who looked down on the commoners and the middle classes but would put brilliantly talented geniuses on a pedestal, even if they weren't on their level financially.

Prince Lichnowsky was so taken with Beethoven that he moved him out of the small attic apartment and into a large apartment on the ground floor. He made sure when Beethoven rang for service that the servants should attend to him instantly. Beethoven was treated like part of the family. It was much more than a musician-patron relationship, and the prince went out of his way to spoil Beethoven. But even though Beethoven appreciated the gifts that he was given and the lifestyle that was lavished upon him, he also felt like he needed to prove himself on his own terms and maintain his independence. So he ended up securing his own servant and bought his own horse, so he wouldn't feel like a burden to the Prince and his family. Instead of eating fancy meals prepared by the Prince's cooks, he would often eat alone at a local tavern to avoid having to get dressed up for dinner.

Innovation would become part of Beethoven's style. And it wasn't just in music. He actually innovated the way that patrons treated artists. Up till then, they were treated as second class citizens. But Beethoven would have none of that. He was known to say to his patron Prince Lichnowsky "What you are, you are by chance and by birth. What I am, I am by myself. There have been, there will be, thousands of princes. There is only one Beethoven."

He also innovated the way audiences listen to music. Before, people would gather to hear music, but it was more like background music, with the audience members playing cards, drinking at the bar, and talking while the musician played. Beethoven would stop and demand that they either sit and listen quietly or they could leave the auditorium. Today, concerts are listened to the same way. Composers in the past would follow certain rules. Beethoven was constantly breaking those rules. People came to hear his music and were always surprised at what they heard. He never gave them what they expected but was always innovating his style and music in general. He was responsible for bridging the gap between the Classical and Romantic styles of performance.

Beethoven was torn between having to sing for his supper and being free to write and play what he wanted. He was the first musician to create his own material and have a patron support it. It had always been established that the patron would decide what kind of art they wanted and would commission the artist to create it. Or the artist's other choices were to get a permanent job as an artist or work as a private teacher. Beethoven wanted the freedom to create on his own. He resented having to create and perform on command like a trained seal, but he knew at times he would have to do it, and he continued to do it for most of his life.

These days all artists have that creative freedom, if they want it. They can get patronage from many places and create the kind of art they want to create. It's up to the patron whether they want to support that artist or not. They can also be hired on commission to create art for patrons, and artists can get hundreds or even thousands of patrons to support their work through crowd-funding.

But just like in the days of Beethoven, artists today still struggle with the right balance of appreciation for patronage and the need for having to be subservient to someone who is paying the bills. It's a contradictory blend of emotions from dependence and independence, to rebelliousness and obedience. Even though he enjoyed the feeling of being a freelance artist, Beethoven often thought about having a permanent position as a musician like his father and grandfather for the security it would give him.

Even as Lichnowsky used his wealth and influence to propel Beethoven's career to new levels, the musician stuck to his guns and avoided being a slave to anyone. If the patron didn't like it, he would find another one. His relationship with Lichnowsky soured when he was asked to play for some visiting French officers. Beethoven refused and stormed out into the night in a thundering rainstorm. Though their friendship was eventually patched up, the financial part never was.

Lichnowsky was a key figure in Beethoven's life for many years, but he wasn't the only one. At one point Beethoven was considering a job as Kapellmeister at the court in Kassel. That's when Archduke Rudolph convinced Prince Kinsky and Prince Lobkowitz to both pay Beethoven a salary that was large enough to keep him in Vienna for the rest of his life. A document showed up one day that read "only one who is free from care can create works of magnitude which are exalted and ennoble art. We have decided to place Herr

Ludwig van Beethoven in a position where the necessities of life shall not clog his powerful genius."

Beethoven was happy to stay in Vienna and turned down the court position in Kassel. But then the Austrian currency became devalued, Kinsky was thrown from a horse and died, and Lobkowitz went bankrupt. It was left to Archduke Rudolph to make sure Beethoven was paid. Beethoven was so grateful that he dedicated more of his compositions to Archduke Rudolph than to anyone else.

Another smart move Beethoven made with patrons was to get them to pay for exclusive subscription rights to his material before anyone else could hear it. Then he dedicated the piece to the nobleman who wanted to impress his friends in the inner circle by being the first patron to have access to it. He would also give patrons exclusive performance rights for a fixed period of time.

Even though Beethoven loved having his creative freedom, this freedom also forced him into the role of entrepreneur and businessman. He became his own agent, manager, attorney, collection agent and distributor. These are some of the roles all entrepreneurial artists must take on. President of Goucher College, Jose Antonio Bowen, makes a great connection between Beethoven and Bill Gates. Bill Gates wrote software for the computer and Beethoven wrote it for the piano. They both had to adapt to change, and they both figured out how to profit from it.

In the 18th century, music was only performed live. It was a social event. If you wanted to hear it, you either had to be wealthy enough to be able to "sponsor" a musician, or you had to go out to see them perform somewhere. But with the invention of sheet music, you could have music in your very own home any time you wanted it, as long as you could play it. And that would require a piano. But, like software, the piano makers would come out with a new model every few months, and that new model would have new features, like extra keys and an extra pedal. The people who got those new piano models were the celebrity musicians of the day.

Beethoven couldn't wait to start writing new music for the new pianos, but other people didn't have them yet and would have to upgrade to a new model if they wanted to play his music. So, there is the similarity between Bill Gates and Beethoven. If Beethoven could have bought stock in those piano companies that really would have increased his personal wealth. But the introduction of sheet music, and much later other new technologies like the radio and the home stereo, would introduce more musicians, and more types of music, to more people around the world.

They say everything that's old is new again. This includes the way music is listened to. Today's millennials weren't around when vinyl records were first popular, but they are embracing them now, accounting for about half of all sales. One reason music fans are listening to vinyl is because it makes the music sound the way the artist intended it to sound. Digital is just a file that is missing the characteristic crackle that can be heard on vinyl records.

When CD technology came on the scene, vinyl records were often converted to CD format without being re-mastered, which means a lot of the original sound quality was lost. Another thing that has been lost is the experience of listening to an entire body of music, again the way an artist intended it to be enjoyed. You can skip tracks on CDs, but it's much harder to do on an album without scratching it. Very few factories even manufacture vinyl records anymore, and the ones that are still around have decades old machinery and a dwindling supply of the material needed to press the records.

Then there are the artists who are following in Beethoven's foot-steps and are innovating their way in the music industry. One innovative artist is the alternative rock singer, songwriter, and producer Beck. His music is multi-faceted and includes shades of rock, funk, soul, country, folk and hip-hop. After releasing several albums, he decided to put out his next album as a book of sheet music called Song Reader. It contained 20 new songs and 100 pages of art. Like Beethoven, he wanted other musicians to play his music, and he has plans to release an album with versions of those songs played by musicians from around the world that were submitted to his website. In 2013 he played three concerts with different guests featuring songs from the Song Reader book.

Another innovative group of music artists is the Scottish rock band Mogwai. They decided to release the song "Tracy" in a tiny metal music box. When you wind the crank on the side, the haunting tune plays. Canadian electronic music producer and performer Joel Thomas Zimmerman, known as DeadMaus5, launched a subscription-based phone app. He was also the first artist who sold an interactive version of an album that allowed listeners to customize the music. The subscription for the phone app is paid as a monthly fee that gives fans access to exclusive music, video, and a behind the scenes look at the dance music star, who is one of the highest paid electronic music producers in the world.

Today there are even more ways for artists and musicians to make money from their work. Technology has leveled the playing field for artists by allowing them to bypass the gatekeepers and become their own distributors. There are a host of new channels to distribute your music as opposed to the days when you would have to be represented by a record company in order to hear your song played on the radio. Distributors like Tunecore, Spotify, Soundcloud, and CD Baby can get your music to digital stores like Amazon, iTunes, Emusic, Rhapsody, Napster, Amazon MP3, Google Play, Pandora, Shazam, Apple Music, YouTube Music, Groove Music, Napster, iHeartRadio, eMusic, Medianet, Tradebit, Slacker, 24-7, 7digital, Deezer, GreatIndieMusic, and MusicNet.

Tunecore is one company that has been turning the old record label business model on its head. The old system was similar to how the book publishing industry works, where an artist would get an advance and the publishing company would put the book together. Record labels would give the artist an advance and then have the album manufactured, get it on store shelves, and make sure it got radio play. Tunecore was started in 2006 by Peter Wells, Jeff Price, and Gary Burke as a way to make sure all artists were able to get their music out whether they had a record label or not. It started as a distribution service to help smaller, indie artists get their music on store shelves. But when record stores went out of business, they had to adjust their plan and set their sights on digital stores. The major difference in business models is that record companies would traditionally keep a large share of the ownership and the money. With Tunecore, the artist pays a flat fee and keeps 100 percent ownership. They also work to get songs on TV and in film.

Spotify is a streaming service for music, podcasts, and videos that was launched in 2008. It is a 'freemium' service which means though basic features are free, additional features, like downloads and ad-free streaming, are available via paid subscriptions. Unlike traditional music sales which are fixed to number of albums sold, Spotify pays artists royalties based on the number of streams. Spotify's tribute driven playlist can drive a new tune to success, much like making the Billboard charts. Spotify doesn't just want to be a place where you go to listen to music. It wants to be the place where you discover music. Your playlist is music you love and want to listen to, but Spotify also wants to introduce you to music you've never heard before, hoping you'll add it to your own playlist.

According to the website MusicBed, there are five ways to make money from your music:

1. Master Use Royalty - The money you get paid every time your music is streamed

2. Mechanical Royalties - This is a royalty you get paid when a copy of your song is made. It originated in the early 20th century because of piano rolls, the common way of recording then.

3. Performance Royalties - Money that is owed to you whenever someone performs your song live.

4. Synchronization - This is when music is paired with visual media. These are usually negotiated on the front end of licensing.

5. Print Royalties - This refers to anything on print, like sheet music. Royalties are paid based on the number of copies made.

Soundcloud is a music sharing service which was founded by sound designer Alexander Ljung and Artist Eric Wahlforss. Ljung is the CEO and Wahlforss is CTO. Users are able to upload, record, promote, and share their originally-created sounds. CD Baby is an online music store that was originally started by musician Derek Sivers to sell his own music. Customers can buy their favorite music as a CD or download. It's one of the few places you can still buy physical CDs.

As an inventor and intellectual property rights owner I believe creativity should be rewarded. If you're going to take the time to create a piece of art of any kind, make sure you protect it. Licensing and royalties are like selling air. Learn the business side of being an artist!

How the Industrial Revolution Changed Art Forever

"The idea of a mass audience was really an invention of the Industrial Revolution."

David Cronenberg

The Industrial Revolution, which started in the United Kingdom in the eighteenth and nineteenth centuries, was a time of giant leaps in manufacturing, mining, transportation, agriculture, and technology. Agricultural societies were transformed into industrial societies. The trend eventually spread to Europe, North America, and the rest of the world. The Industrial Revolution had a major impact on every aspect of society. Technology and innovation forever changed the way business was done and brought about a growing and permanent middle class. People were now moving into the cities to be closer to their jobs or traveling into them via new forms of transportation like the subway and railroad to work in the factories.

The changes during this time period were exciting, scary, progressive, and confusing, all at the same time. Most people saw their incomes increase as the demand for labor increased. But not everyone profited. Skilled artisans who once had made a good living were suddenly put out of business. Art was forever changed as machines replaced the craftsmen system and brought about cheaper and faster mass production. The lowered cost of art supplies meant more artists were able to paint and sculpt, and more paintings were being created to keep up with the growing demand.

For the first time, artists began copying their own works, and collectors not only weren't bothered by it, they encouraged it. They claimed that the reproduction was actually even more valuable because they had more experience as an artist when they made the copies. They said they were the new and improved versions. Even collectors who could easily afford to buy an original would pay full price for a copy. The new art collectors didn't have a problem owning a painting that was also owned by other people because art took on more spiritual and educational value. One of a kind originality wasn't as important as it had been in the past. The elite wouldn't have wanted to have the same picture hanging on their wall as their neighbor, just like celebrities today don't want to show up on the red carpet wearing the same dress as someone else. But the majority of the population wasn't concerned about that, just like the majority of women today will buy a dress that has been mass produced from a department store. These days we wouldn't think twice about seeing artwork on the packaging for a consumer product. But up until the 1800s that just wasn't something that was done when Thomas Barratt, chairman of the soap company A & F Pears, decided it would be a good way to sell his soap. As he once said "Any fool can make soap. It takes a clever man to sell it." Barratt broke new ground when he purchased the rights to John Evert Millais' painting of a young boy titled "Bubbles." He then had a bar of Pears soap painted on the picture and reproduced it in art poster style for mass production. Barratt has been called "the father of modern advertising." He created slogans and phrases for his soap products to get the word out. The Pears soap brand was the world's first legally registered brand.

He also held an annual Miss Pears competition to find a "spokes model" who could be used on the soap packages and in advertising promotions. He was also the first person to use celebrity endorsement, hiring scientists and celebrities of the day. British singer and actor Lille Langtry was the first woman to endorse Pears soap. The new style caught on in the United States and companies like Coca Cola and Campbell's soup were soon commissioning the talents of artists like Norman Rockwell to do the same for their brands.

Barratt's competition, William Hesketh Lever of Lever Bros., also wanted to get in on the 'high art as consumer product' bandwagon. He bought the rights to "The New Frock" by William Powell Frith to promote his brand Sunlight Soap, which he turned into a reproducible image. Frith wasn't pleased when Lever added the phrase "So clean" to the reproduction, but there was nothing he could do since Lever had bought the copyright to the picture. Lever made this quote about advertising: "I know half my advertising isn't working. I just don't know which half."

One important invention of the Industrial Revolution was lithography. It was the first new method of printing in over three hundred years. Lithography used chemical processes to create an image. Like many other inventions throughout history, lithography was invented by accident. Bavarian playwright Alois Senefelder figured out that he could duplicate his scripts by writing them in crayon on slabs of limestone and then printing them with rolled-on ink. He invented the technique of printing with stone plates, which improved upon the old method of materials such as maps having to be hand drawn and engraved. The old hand drawn artwork was expensive and time consuming, but the new method cut the time and expense and revolutionized the printing industry.

Lithography started out as a single-color printing method. In 1837 a French printer patented a new process of color printing called chromolithography, which changed the world of advertising. This enabled an artist to create mass produced color posters, illustrated books, catalogs, and other types of advertising materials, like the Victorian trade cards used by tradesmen to advertise their products. Art and trade were beginning to merge into the business of advertising, which has expanded opportunities for artists in all mediums and continues to this day.

Photography was another invention that revolutionized the art world. It was invented by the French painter Louis Mande Daguerre, who wasn't just an inventor, he was also an innovator. His first innovation was called the diorama, a theatrical viewing of a painting in a highly specialized theater. The entire show only lasted about fifteen minutes, during which time the painting would slowly and dramatically change. Multi-layered panels in the painting would be lit from behind, while the entire audience rotated on a massive turntable, creating a stunning illusion.

Daguerre's fascination with light and optical illusions would eventually lead him to a process known as daguerreotype, the beginning of what we now know as photography. It was similar to our modern day Polaroid film. Photography changed the way we saw the world and the way artists painted it. No longer was a painting just the personal interpretation of what the artist saw. Time was literally "frozen" so the artist could capture a real moment in time like a horse in mid gallop or a person in action.

Innovation was ubiquitous during the Industrial Revolution. Victorian artists started experimenting with different styles, techniques, non-traditional materials, and vibrant colors. Instead of just pleasing one patron, they were now starting to appeal to a more mass audience. The working class favored a different style of art than the landed gentry elite. And as the working class had more money, they were able to demand the kind of art they enjoyed.

People could now travel greater distances around the world and they could do it in less time. This enabled artists to experience different cultures and bring back new ideas that led to more innovation in art, like those Impressionist artists who traveled the world seeking new cultural inspiration.

At first the elite didn't notice that the middle-class patrons were changing the art schools and public galleries to fit their own tastes. By the time they figured it out, it was too late. The middle-class, art buying public had already put their foot down about what kind of art they wanted to see and hang in their homes. They had changed art culture forever. It was no longer extra large images of religious figures or massive battles; now it was more likely smaller tableaus, like a working man and his dog or children picking flowers in a field. Working people wanted to buy art they could relate to, which included images of themselves instead of pictures of priests, rulers, or the elite. For the first time, the middle class working people had art that gave them something to model themselves after and to aspire to, that fit their own tastes and fit into the decor of their own homes.

As the demand for labor increased, the lower classes started earning more money and now had more expendable income to buy things like art. Since art was an investment as well as a symbol of wealth, more middle class people were able to own it. This created a high demand for art dealers. Many of the dealers were specializing in a particular style of art. Because of the number of different styles that came out of that period, there were more ways for dealers to make money, and more artists to manage.

The Industrial Revolution was a time of extreme creativity and innovation. High art was forever fractured, and the amount of low art in the market multiplied. Numerous movements were created that either included the social aspects of the industrial age or fought against them. The Romantic movement fought against the machine and revived an interest in the Middle Ages. More emphasis was placed on emotions than on reason. Romantics yearned for a simpler time before industrialization when they could be surrounded by nature and spiritual learning. Romantic artists wanted to capture these feelings in their art, which included a lot of landscapes and scenes of nature. They were much more likely to pursue art simply for art's sake.

An offshoot of the Romantic movement was the Pre-Raphaelite Brotherhood, who shared a distrust for the sanctioned art institution of the day, the Royal Academy. It was from this movement that the inspiration for the Arts and Crafts movement was born. New artists joined in and the Pre-Raphaelite movement merged into the Aesthetic movement, which supported aesthetic values over social-political themes. The artists of this movement believed art should be about beauty and pleasure rather than art that conveyed moral or political messages. Many artists of the Aesthetic movement believed in the personal relationships they could have with patrons. They had fought for the right to be treated as equals by their patrons. The Realism movement was started to push back against Romanticism. It was grounded in reality and favored showing things the way they were. The scenes in Realist paintings lacked emotions and highlighted social conditions.

The Impressionist movement started with 55 artists whose work had been rejected by the French state-sponsored exhibition called the Salon. It was the only chance artists had of getting their work seen and sold. So they decided to stage their own independent exhibition for the public. The Impressionist artists broke every rule of the old traditional way that had been taught by the conservative French Academy of Fine Arts. Their work was a precursor to modern art and was panned by critics, who didn't understand the new style. Often the Impressionists were painting outside, directly from nature, which was more possible now that paint was now sold in small, portable tubes which allowed artists to leave their studios and go out into nature.

Outside of folk songs, much music, like art, was enjoyed by the elite only. Musicians were hired by either the court or by the church and were thought of as servants. But during the Industrial Revolution, the middle classes wanted to participate too. The invention of new musical instruments and the ability to manufacture them in volume and in good quality was an open door for the middle class to start taking music lessons and to spend some of their discretionary income on live performances.

Because of the expanded outlets for musicians, more were able to make a good living with their craft. The ones who could put on dazzling and dramatic live performances in large theaters and parlors were able to command a lot of money and become the first musical super stars. Musicians went from being low-class servants catering to the wealthy to the independent celebrities of their time. They traveled throughout Europe, and their fame grew.

Music was played in both large concert halls and in small, intimate parlors. Musicians were now able to support themselves performing in both. The invention of the piano was a game-changing innovation. It became the center of family entertainment, and small groups of people would be invited to a home to listen to piano music. Some musicians, like Frederic Chopin were able to make a very good living playing the parlor circuit with the help of a patron.

As music became more popular, symphonic and operatic works grew in scale. Orchestras got bigger and accommodated more instruments. Larger and louder violins replaced the quieter ones. The guitar, harp, and banjo became popular. The only instrument that got smaller was the piano, so it could fit into the space of the average home.

The literary industry was vastly changed during the Industrial Revolution through innovation. One of the most innovative and successful writers of the Victorian era was Charles Dickens. He grew up in poverty and vowed that he would someday get out of it, which he did. He took advantage of the new capitalist revolution and became an extremely successful entrepreneur. But he never forgot where he came from, using his childhood as fodder for most of his novels.

Dickens had perfect timing, writing during an era with so many industrial innovations happening at once. The old hand-operated printing press was replaced by the new steam-powered rubber plate rotary press and enabled printing to be done on an industrial scale. Suddenly the output of the old press was doubled, as was the size of the printed area. Innovations in transportation also meant books could be distributed more easily and to greater distances. First coaches made that possible, and, eventually, railroads would speed things along.

Dickens used the development of magazine wholesalers to his advantage and invented a new concept—writing in serial format. His first successful serial publication was "The Pickwick Papers." It launched a line of merchandise, which included figurines, song books, playing cards, puzzles, boot polish, candy tins, and cigars. He wrote his last novel, "Our Mutual Friend," in twenty installments. It also allowed him to get feedback from his audience along the way and modify the plot and character development based on what the audience thought was more important.

He invented the devise of the cliffhanger to keep the audience in suspense. In fact, his method was similar to today's soap operas where the primary characters are covered in the plot, then he would switch to subplots that involved other characters. Novels had never been published in serial format before. Writers used to get paid on the royalty system, which meant they would have to wait for their money until after the book was written, published, and sold to collect what was owed them. This would forever change the way authors sold their work and would pave the way for future writers. One of the benefits of doing it this way was that he could get paid along the way while he was writing the novel and avoid ever being without money.

Dickens published his books with expensive bindings for people who could afford it and cheaper bindings for people who couldn't. He didn't want the poor to not have access to his writing. The messages in his books resonated with people of all classes. Like many writers, Dickens worked freelance and often had trouble paying his bills. One Christmas proved to be especially difficult and creditors were knocking at the door. He wrote "A Christmas Carol" to make enough money to at least pay down some of the debt. When his publisher turned it down, he took the small amount of money he had and self-published it.

He retained his publisher as the printers of the book only and then gave them a percentage of the sales. Dickens not only wrote the book in time for Christmas but hired the illustrator, oversaw the book design, and did all of the marketing, just as writers are able to do now. "A Christmas Carol" turned out to be an even bigger hit than expected. And since Dickens put his own money into it, he was able to keep 100 percent of the profits. To this day, "A Christmas Carol" has never been out of print, and its timely message of giving from your heart never goes out of style.

He was also a pioneer in sponsorship for writers. His installment novels were sponsored by brands that were advertised at the beginning and end of the books. Because of rising consumerism in Victorian England during the Industrial Revolution, brands were looking for unique ways to advertise their goods, and the most famous man in England at the time had the perfect way to do that. He used brilliant color ads to sell umbrellas, insect powder, jewelry, and glasses.

Besides being an author, Dickens was also a performer. In fact, it had always been his true passion next to writing. He had always been an amateur actor. He wrote his first play at the age of six and played the leading role, along with directing it. Even though he became successful as a writer, acting was still his true love. He returned to the stage to do readings of his work, which were a huge hit. They were staged as polished theatrical productions where he played all of the roles. Like as was true in his novels, the audience was kept on the edge of their seats. Dickens loved the thrill of performing for his fans, who loved him. His last tour was sponsored, and he brought in a lot of money from his speaking fees and from books.

He gave his all, touring despite doctor's orders to quit, until his health simply gave out. Unlike many of his fellow writers, Dickens died a wealthy man. His novels have never gone out of print, and over 200 movie and TV adaptations have been completed.

❧

The artist-patron relationship was about to shift from subservience to greater independence; artists became more entrepreneurial as they realized they no longer needed a single patron to pay their bills. As more and more merchants rose in social status and started collecting more art, there were simply more patrons to choose from. The size of the art world in England was expanding quickly. And more new up and coming artists were getting a chance to make a living with their skills. Artists often became tough negotiators with patrons and had learned how to promote themselves through the press and with self-advertising, many to the point of becoming wealthy celebrities in the process.

One of those wealthy celebrities was William Powell Frith. Frith was one of the most successful artists in British history. He became the equivalent of a multi-millionaire by creating art that could be enjoyed by the masses to reach the biggest audience possible. His paintings were painted parables of good and evil through scenes of everyday life. He took advantage of the new prosperity of the Industrial Revolution and became a shrewd entrepreneur businessman, sometimes refusing to name a price until a piece was complete, haggling over commissions.

As it was a seller's market, artists were less likely to compromise and took on the attitude of the 'artist as genius.' They started seeing themselves as being members of a separate class, and some, like Dante Gabriel Rosetti, even seeing themselves as being in a separate class from ordinary humans. Rosetti had demeaning names for patrons who disagreed with him, and he labeled himself as a genius.

Another demanding and temperamental artist was the painter James McNeil Whistler, of "Whistler's Mother" fame. He believed that art was not to be used as a morality tale for social purposes and terrorized anyone who disagreed with him. He sued the art critic John Ruskin after he blasted his "Nocturne in Black and Gold" painting in a review that made him look like a fraud. One of his patrons was shipping magnate Frederick R. Leyland. While away on business, Leyland asked Whistler to paint something minor for his porcelain display case. Whistler got carried away and painted a huge mural of peacocks without permission. To add insult to injury, he invited friends and the press over to view it before Leyland got home. Then when he came back, Whistler handed him a huge bill for the work. Leyland was furious and a battle ensued over the issue.

Even though people like Irish painter James Barry would publicly denounce artists who were corrupted by money, many artists were able to balance their sense of creating art for a higher purpose with the capitalist view of creating art for money. Even the greatest artists of the time started focusing on making money from their art. It was now becoming acceptable. And as more artists saw that it was possible to make large sums of money being an artist, more artists entered the market. Like artists today, it became a rivalry between professional artists and amateurs.

Today professional artists or amateurs can become a You Tube or reality show star overnight and make millions doing it. As long as they have enough fans who want to see them, it doesn't really matter if someone is a celebrity or an average Joe sitting in his parents' basement talking about how much they like video games. Since You Tube launched in 2015, it has been creating video millionaires through sponsored content. The performances range from sports commentary, comedy, and video gaming to cooking and makeup videos.

Producer/writer/directors Benny and Rafi Fine created something called the React video series. The brothers show viral videos to people and film their reactions. They've been sponsored by Ford and Comedy Central. When Lindsey Stirling couldn't get signed to a record label, she started posting her videos to YouTube. Now the classically trained violinist has become known as the "hip-hop violinist" because of her violin versions of hip-hop songs. This is an example of an artist with enormous talent who just couldn't break into the business by going in the traditional door but now is one of the highest paid musicians on You Tube, bringing in around $6 million in 2015. Not bad for a performer who was told she was "unmarketable."

Comedians Rhett and Link are wildly popular on You Tube as, according to their website, "Internetainers." They have a daily internet talk show and an award-winning weekly podcast. Their channels have over 20 million subscribers with a total view count of over 4 billion. They've become known for making comedic ads for real, local companies and have received corporate sponsorship.

༄

Like today, Victorian artists knew anyone could be an artist if they wanted to be, and anyone could be a critic, just like someone today might rate a movie on Red Box or write a book review on Amazon. Professional artists in the Victorian era realized that they had to become more business savvy if they wanted to compete with the new amateurs. And, just like today, there were more ways than ever for an artist to make money, including opening their own studios as galleries. They could sell through a dealer or direct to the public. They could put on public shows and private shows and make as little or as much as they could get for their work.

Once the nouveau riche had capitalized on the steam engine and subsequent mechanical innovations and had made their wealth, they turned to art both as a place of retreat from the stress of business and a way to secure their place in society alongside the landed gentry. They felt that they had finally arrived and could now compete with the elite. Businessmen like William Graham had everything money could buy. He was surrounded by material wealth and a loving family, yet turned to art to fill a void that was still missing in his life. Like today, the patronage of art wasn't always just about the material return on investment. Patrons also sponsor art for social status, the experience of being a part of something bigger, and having the ability to share in the creative process.

Art patrons also tended to patronize more than one artist. And, unlike patrons of the past, they didn't usually invite artists to live in their homes or fix them up with eligible women for marriage. They also didn't interfere with their personal lives as some earlier patrons had done. But the new artists on the scene might still be invited to private parties, and they took advantage of an expanded social life in new circles.

Like the dilettantes, many aesthetic collectors were artists themselves. Founder of the pharmaceutical society, Jacob Bell, was one of them. In art class he mocked the teacher when asked to draw a large plaster ball. The teacher told him "Your father placed you here for the purpose of making an artist of you. I can't do it. I can make nothing of you." Though Bell didn't achieve his father's dream of him becoming an artist, he did go on to be a significant presence in the art world by becoming a patron and advisor to other artists. He commissioned their work, advised them in business matters, and created a social environment for them to network with other art aficionados.

New markets of art buyers brought about a new business model for selling art—the dealer-run commercial art gallery. Art critics and editors would become educational conduits between the art world and the public. Examples were Tom Taylor of the *Times*, and Samuel Carter Hall of the *Art Journal*.

The most influential art critic of the day was John Ruskin. Ruskin was also a painter, patron, and philanthropist, making him a dilettante as well. As a regular reviewer of the art exhibitions at the Royal Academy, it was widely known that he could either make or break an artist's career. He wanted the price of art to be low and based on the actual time spent on the piece. He also believed art should have moral value.

Today's consumers still want to buy mass produced artwork, but some modern artists have figured out how to mass produce commissioned oil paintings with human hands instead of machines. One company that does this is called Instapainting. Customers send in photos that they want turned into oil paintings. These were often family portraits, pet pictures, and pictures of the family home. And it was all done on canvas for less than $100. In the beginning they started out selling a couple of dozen, but as orders got bigger, they realized they would have to find a way to do more paintings faster. That's when they found out about a little village in China called Dafen. Over 8,000 painters reside in Dafen and it has become a human oil painting factory to the tune of around $100 million dollars. Painters spend their days reproducing artwork by hand to be sold at budget prices. In fact, the majority of mass produced oil paintings come from that one village.

Another example of modern day artists who are making a living from handmade art is the website Etsy. According to their website, "Etsy is a marketplace where people around the world connect, both online and offline, to make, sell, and buy unique goods." Etsy was started as a community where crafters could sell their work, and fans could buy one of a kind pieces they couldn't find in stores.

Their timing was perfect because the female crafting movement was just taking hold. Etsy capitalized on it by getting out into the communities and connecting with people at craft fairs, convincing them to sell their handmade products on Etsy. They targeted the influential artists, hoping they would become successful and encourage other artists to do the same. Those artists had a substantial following offline but hadn't ventured into online commerce yet, so they were motivated to send people to the site. Word of mouth spread and Etsy took off.

Just like technological advances disrupted art during the Industrial Revolution, the digital age is also disrupting art, bringing with it new markets and innovation for a new generation of artists. The Internet allows artists to bypass the old gatekeepers and go directly to the fans that appreciate their art, whether it's fine art, performing art, or literary art.

Barriers to entry have always favored those established institutions, like large publishing houses, movie studios, and record companies, who had the money and name recognition to keep competitors out. But business savvy artists can now create their own empires if they are willing to work hard behind the scenes, on top of rising to the top of their craft. But low barriers to entry also create an enormous amount of competitors, which is why artists today must figure out how to carve out their own distinct personae in a sea of similar artists.

Arts and Entertainment in the American Industrial Revolution

"Greed is good."

Gordon Gekko

Just as the Industrial Revolution changed England forever, so would the American Industrial Revolution change every aspect of American life. The innovative products and processes that came out of it made life easier and work more efficient. Jobs were plentiful and wages nearly doubled from 1870 to 1900. Wealth, GDP, real wages, and capital formation were all increasing rapidly. This new era of inventions and innovations would also change all areas of art, from the fine arts to literary arts to performing arts. The inventions and innovations of the new industrialized America, such as the telephone, radio, TV and the electric light, are still continuing to this day.

The Gilded Age was a culturally and intellectually dynamic time as museums and libraries sprang up everywhere. Associations such as the American Historical Association and the American Library

Association were formed. Innovations in communications, transportation, electrical power, and the oil, steel, natural gas, and aluminum industries made it possible to expand through mass production.

Suddenly there was an America, which had always been rural and agrarian, becoming urban and industrial. Workers flocked to the cities, and tens of millions of immigrants poured into the country for a chance at the American Dream. Hard working entrepreneurs took advantage of the opportunities available because of the railroads and telephone lines that were stretched across the country, along with cheaper labor and cost of goods.

The nouveau riche and middle classes wanted to flaunt their riches through extravagant surroundings and lavish lifestyles. This included art in all forms. Just like in the Middle Ages, art patronage and philanthropy were ways to accomplish that. Wealthy Americans had a fascination with European design, and many artists went to study with the masters in Europe. James McNeil Whistler and John Singer Sargent were well known portrait painters who both moved to England to study. The new millionaires in America wanted to adorn their mansions with their own portraits, so their images could be captured for posterity. One of the most famous painters of the era was Winslow Homer. He was especially known for his powerful paintings of the New England coastline. But when he didn't have steady patrons, he struggled financially, which began to wear on him as an artist. Many of his steady patrons were family and friends.

But because of mass production, art was no longer just for the wealthy, and it was no longer just about paintings. The burgeoning middle class adorned their homes with art of all kinds. The interior design market was just getting started, and stained glass, rugs, and furniture were now also included under the banner of "art." The middle class filled their homes with bric a brac, worthless chochkes like tea cups, vases, porcelain figurines, painted eggshells, and bunches of artificial flowers that they kept in curio cabinets. They imitated the rich as best they could as their own income increased.

The wealthy Americans of that time didn't really have their own culture, so they borrowed from the French. Everything was French. They ate French food, drank French wine, and hung French artwork in their extravagant homes. American artists were only worth their time if they had studied abroad or had wealth and social status of their own. The artists who did very well for themselves knew that art was a business and they treated it as such. They knew that if they wanted to get ahead and avoid going down the path of the starving or struggling artist, having a patron was the best way to do it.

Eventually artists and patrons would form a bond to establish their own American culture, even if borrowed from cultures around the world. Artists would often travel with their patrons to other countries, picking up bits and pieces of international flair to incorporate into their own work.

The wealthy wanted to show off their great fortunes and did everything they could to outdo each other, building huge mansions and riding in gold-trimmed carriages. The more money they could waste on gaudy trinkets, the better their standing in social circles. Their homes often had numerous rooms and included art galleries, theaters, and libraries. They would cover every wall of their homes until their collections grew to be too big for their houses.

More free time and disposable income meant both wealthy and ordinary Americans alike wanted a variety of pastimes. Prior to the Gilded Age, entertainment such as folk festivals, 4th of July celebrations, and parades were popular. But Americans began to crave more diverse entertainment. In the nineteenth century America started transitioning from heavily influenced theater, and especially English theater, to developing its own style. Burlesques, minstrel shows, circuses, comic operas, honky tonk, Wild West shows, vaudeville, and musicals became popular. The Gilded Age gave birth to many new types of entertainment. One of the most well-known raconteurs of that time was P.T. Barnum. After several failed attempts at business, he went to New York City without a penny to his name and began his career as a showman. He quickly realized he had a knack for discovering unusual talent.

It started with an elderly slave named Joice Heth. Barnum believed she was actually 161 years old and sold that illusion to the public. She enjoyed entertaining, and made a decent living in Barnum's show. If the public really believed she was 161, so be it. After her death, an autopsy revealed she was probably not even 80. It was then that Barnum learned that the public enjoyed being deceived, as long as they were also being entertained. This fueled his drive to remain in the business he coined "show business."

Barnum founded an inexpensive form of entertainment for the working class—the dime museum. The first one, called the "American Museum", was founded by Barnum in New York City. It was billed as edutainment for the masses, a lowbrow combination of entertainment and moral education. It included freaks shows, wax figures, films, variety acts, melodramas, and pseudo-scientific exhibits. He would take his troupe of human oddities on the road, and eventually created the Barnum Show, which was his grandest show ever. This would later become the Barnum & Bailey Circus and would be seen by crowds all over the world.

Traveling shows had to appeal to a mass audience and that usually meant variety shows. The performers in these shows had to be versatile both on stage and off, such as stars like John Durang, who was an actor, singer, dancer, clown, tightrope walker and puppeteer. When he was off stage he would do tasks like painting and moving scenery.

The variety show broke off into two different directions, vaudeville and burlesque. Vaudeville started out as mostly bawdy acts for male audiences but eventually branched out to become more of a family-friendly type of entertainment, including opera singers, magicians, animal acts, dancers, comedians, and classical musicians. Singer and entertainer Tony Pastor went from producing variety shows to creating the first vaudeville show in a theater he leased in New York City. Burlesque started out as a form of comedy and music frequented by the working class that made fun of the social habits of the upper class. But after a production called "The Black Crook," a racy musical featuring scantily clad women in skin-colored tights, burlesque became a type of entertainment known for more explicit material.

Vaudeville and burlesque performers would travel around the country playing "the circuit." From the mid to late nineteenth century, actors and performers took advantage of the transcontinental railroad and went on tours across America. An actor/manager would put together tours that would play for several weeks in one city, then move on to the next.

But this would all change after a chance meeting between six men over lunch: John Zimmerman, Sr., Charles Frohman, Samuel Nixon, Al Hayman, Marc Klaw, and A.L. Erlanger. Collectively they owned a large number of theaters across the country. In an attempt to dominate the theater scene, they formed the Theatrical Syndicate, or The Syndicate as it was known. Then the Syndicate unified their group of theaters and standardized the entire booking process. The manager was cut out of the process because The Syndicate handled all management. Theater companies were pressured into turning a profit or risk being dropped from the list. The shows were wildly popular and made an enormous amount of money for The Syndicate, which was only interested in the biggest and most commercial productions to take on the road.

Actors were also pressured by The Syndicate and had to abide by their strict rules or risk not working at all. Many tried to fight them but ended up having to give in to their many demands. In the 1880s the star system became a way to attract bigger crowds and higher admission prices. Actors were identified with certain roles, and innovation and experimentation took a back seat to a proven, successful strategy that was guaranteed to bring in money. JJ and Lee Shubert eventually broke the monopoly after buying enough theaters to create competition. Soon, actors and other theater professionals jumped ship and joined the Shuberts, bringing an end to a decade-long reign by The Syndicate. The traveling variety shows would soon be disrupted by the invention of moving pictures. Suddenly the same people who plunked down money for live shows wanted to see movie stars on the big screen.

❧

The biggest patrons of the Gilded Age were the titans of industry. These were men like John D. Rockefeller, Andrew Carnegie, J. P. Morgan, Leland Stanford, T. B. Walker, and Cornelius Vanderbilt. Though some of their critics complained that they were robber barons, making their vast fortunes on the backs of the workers, many others, artists included, were the happy recipients of their generous philanthropy, which continues to this day.

One of the largest art galleries of the time was owned by lumber baron T.B. Walker. His vast collection eventually outgrew his home and he built a gallery, which doubled in size through the years. It was open to the public at no charge every day except Sundays and holidays. Unlike many wealthy collectors back then, Walker's collection was open to the public, and anyone who knocked on his front door could have access to the artworks, which were hung in the main house. No invitation was necessary.

Shipping and railroad magnate Cornelius Vanderbilt was known more as an art collector than a direct patron who commissioned it. The Vanderbilt mansion was known for its lavish balls, which included the who's who list of the elite social circles of New York's Gilded Age crowd. His home art gallery was also open to the public. Sort of. It was only open on Thursdays between 11 and 4 and only if you happened to have a personal invitation. The gallery was cordoned off from the rest of the home and had its own entrance.

Steel magnate Andrew Carnegie was one of the most high profile philanthropists of his time and gave away 90 percent of his fortune in his lifetime. He encouraged other wealthy Americans to follow him in giving their money away to help improve society.

Carnegie was a true self-made man whose rags to riches story started off in Scotland, where his family had fallen on hard times and the rest of the country was in starvation. His family moved to America for a chance at a better life. Little Andrew made $1.20 a week working in a cotton factory.

But Carnegie was a hard worker and a quick learner. He made connections with all of Pittsburgh's business owners and read every book he could get his hands on. Years later when he started making money, he always gave a portion of it away to charity. He believed that part of life was accumulating wealth and the other part was distributing that wealth through philanthropic causes. He believed that everyone should be able to participate in art and culture and not just the privileged few. He supported art, theater, and music, and donated the prize money for the Carnegie International, a showcase of contemporary art.

Carnegie was also a dilettante and wrote three books on travel. He believed that books were powerful and that everyone should have access to them. He built over 2500 libraries and gave millions to educational institutions. It was the wealthy industrialist's love of music and a chance encounter with a conductor and musical director that launched one of the greatest icons of music—Carnegie Hall. Andrew Carnegie and his new wife Louise were on a ship headed for Scotland to begin their honeymoon. Walter Damrosch, musical director of the Symphony Society of New York, was going to Scotland to study when he struck up a friendship with the Carnegies. Damrosch talked about his vision for a new concert hall in New York City that would be self-sustaining and would bring the greatest artists in the world to its stage and set the standard for music. Carnegie, a music lover himself, jumped at the chance to fund it and be a part of musical history. From Tchaikovsky's appearance on opening night, Carnegie Hall has led the way in musical excellence, all thanks to the generous patronage of its founder, Andrew Carnegie.

John Pierpont Morgan was a powerhouse in the banking and

finance industry. He also took over Andrew Carnegie's steel company (without lawyers or contracts) and merged it with the Federal Steel Company, along with having investments in the railroad industry. Like other titans of industry, J.P. Morgan was a huge philanthropist. In his lifetime he gave away all but 19 percent of his new worth to charity. An avid art lover and collector, he was a benefactor of the American Museum of Art and the American Museum of Natural History.

Turn of the century photographer Edward S. Curtis embarked on a thirty-year journey to document the trials and tribulations of the American Indian. He wanted to create a photographic study that would be put into twenty limited edition, leather bound books called "The American Indian." In a national portrait contest, Curtis took first place among 18,000 entrants. This caught the attention of then President Theodore Roosevelt who wrote him a letter of recommendation. Curtis used that letter to approach J. P. Morgan for financing. Morgan agreed to put in some backing. But the project took way more time and money than had been anticipated, and Curtis had to hold it together on his own. "The American Indian" is now known as one of the most important historical references on the culture of the American Indian.

J. P. Morgan, along with Cornelius Vanderbilt, Jay Gould, and Louis C. Tiffany, backed the Casino Theater in New York. It was considered a risky move, as it was located sixteen blocks north of the theater district. Rudolph Aronson created it as a venue for musicals and operetta. The Casino was responsible for introducing the chorus line to America and started the trend of girl revues.

Leland Stanford was a New York based attorney until his brothers convinced him there was gold in California. In those days before easy transportation, Leland had to take a steamship down the eastern coastline, get off in Panama, then cross the mountains before taking another steamship up the western coastline. The whole trip would take at least a month. Little did Stanford know it at the time, but he would one day become the governor of California and the president of the first intercontinental railroad, which would revolutionize travel in the United States.

Stanford soon discovered that the gold rush wasn't the easy money he thought it would be and changed courses. He decided to be the one selling tools and supplies to the miners, who just couldn't give up on their dream until they struck it rich or exhausted their options. Stanford got rich the slow and steady way. He and his wife Jane loved living the high life. They had the biggest, most extravagant home money could buy, and they needed a photographer to document it all.

That's when they met Edward Muybridge, an entrepreneurial artist who traveled in a wagon he called The Flying Studio, which had a complete darkroom and allowed him the freedom to photograph what he loved the most—nature. He used a one name moniker, Helios, before icons like Cher, Madonna, and Prince made it fashionable and was prone to changing his name at least every ten years.

Muybridge became known for his quick turnaround time and was able to capture the worst earthquake San Francisco had ever experienced by being the first one in the street; he was also able to process the pictures quickly in The Flying Studio. Within a week he had a whole series of earthquake photos in stores around town. As an entrepreneurial artist out on his own, he was always searching for new niche markets where he could make money. The market for pictures of American Indians was just starting to take off, and "Helios" jumped on the bandwagon.

The photographer was also an inventor, patenting something he called the Sky Shade. It was a device that blocked some of the bright blue light of the sky when he photographed clouds, and it avoided washout on the picture's negative. Stanford soon became the eccentric photographer's patron. Their shared love of horses would cement the relationship, even though it was an odd and frequently strained one. It was ironic that Stanford's railroad would eventually replace the horse-drawn carriage as the means of long distance travel.

Muybridge is considered the first person to make what came to be called "moving pictures." He was commissioned by Sanford to photograph his beloved horses in motion. Stanford paid for all of the equipment, assistants, and anything else he needed to make the project a success. Everything except a salary. Muybridge eventually invented a projection device called the zoopraxiscope, which laid the groundwork for the motion picture industry. He later traveled around the country speaking at universities, demonstrating his invention.

The Rockefeller family has one of the greatest legacies in America as patrons of the arts. John D. Rockefeller, Sr. was one of the richest men in the world. He passed down to his son John D., Jr., not only his great wealth, but his view of philanthropy, which was to give away as much of your money as possible. If he donated money, he wanted to be very sure that it was going to go to a good cause. When John D. Rockefeller married Abby Greene Aldrich, the two became an art powerhouse. Unlike her husband, she favored modern art, and was a co-founder of the Museum of Modern Art, which would become one of the most influential museums of modern art in the world. John was initially opposed to the museum but later became one of its greatest benefactors. It opened to the public just nine days after the stock market crash of 1929.

The Rockefellers commissioned a lot of artists, especially during the Depression. Rockefeller Center was built at the peak of the Great Depression. Its nineteen commercial buildings cover twenty-two acres in Midtown Manhattan. Thirty artists were commissioned to work on it at a time when most artists were struggling. One of those artists was Mexican painter Diego Rivera. His relationship with his patrons, the Rockefellers, was a very interesting partnership, especially since he was an avowed Communist and the Rockefellers were decidedly Capitalists. Rivera was commissioned to paint "Man at the Crossroads" for the Rockefeller Center. It was controversial because it included an image of Lenin. The picture was destroyed before it was completed.

The Rockefeller legacy included the Museum of Modern Art

(MoMA), the Metropolitan Museum of Art, the Cloisters, Lincoln Center, Rockefeller Center, Riverside Church, and the Museum of the Oriental Art at the University of Chicago. They not only commissioned art, donated art, and funded museums, but they left the world a new appreciation for art itself.

⮹

The Gilded Age in America was also a time of great change in the literary world. By the mid nineteenth century, America was one of the largest publishers of literature in the world.

Samuel Langhorne Clemens, aka Mark Twain, was one of the most famous writers of the Gilded Age, capturing the American spirit with characters such as Tom Sawyer and Huckleberry Finn. In fact, he is the one who coined the phrase "gilded age" in his satirical book "The Gilded Age: A Tale of Today" about the greed and political corruption in post-Civil War America. Twain was a brilliant writer but a terrible businessman. He had some success with his first book "The Gilded Age," which received favorable reviews and an invention he got a patent for, a self-pasting scrapbook. The self-pasting scrapbook worked a little like an envelope because it used a dried adhesive on the pages where you would moisten it and stick a picture. He came up with the idea because he would keep scrapbooks of his travels, filled with articles and press about his books, souvenirs, and pictures.

Twain also had two other inventions. One was the "Improvement in Adjustable and Detachable Straps for Garments" and a history trivia game. But the self-pasting scrapbook was the only invention he made money with. It ended up making Twain around $50,000. Then he decided to start his own publishing company, which he named Charles L. Webster, after his nephew and co-owner. Under the new banner he published "The Adventures of Huckleberry Finn" and a biography of President Ulysses S. Grant. After struggling with the publishing company for ten long years, it finally went under. He was introduced to industrialist and financier Henry Huttleston Rogers through a mutual friend. Huttleston made his fortune in the oil industry and was a leader at Standard Oil. Huttleston would go on to become a good friend and a guardian angel patron to Twain in his later years.

One of the most influential poets of the Gilded Age was Walt Whitman. He was also an essayist and journalist. His poetry style would earn him the label "the father of free verse." His writing career started in journalism, where he was the editor of a prominent New York newspaper, the *Brooklyn Daily Eagle*. In 1848 he started his own newspaper called the *Brooklyn Freeman*. Several years later he continued his entrepreneurial career as a writer by self-publishing his first book of poetry, the infamous *Leaves of Grass*. The style was a stark departure from the mainstream poetic norm at the time. He published 795 copies of the book, which was all he could afford. Self-published books were a common practice back in the nineteenth century and were on the same level as a book published by a publishing house today.

Walt Whitman had several patrons who supported him throughout his career. One was Anne Burrows Gilchrist, a writer from England who had fallen madly in love with Whitman after reading *Leaves of Grass*. She moved to America to be close to him, bringing her children with her. They never consummated a romantic relationship but ended up becoming the best of friends until the day she died. She was passionate about him as a writer and raised funds for him so he could continue to write.

Another supporter was the European editor and critic, William Rossetti. After reading an article about Whitman's financial problems he rallied friends to donate money and to subscribe to Whitman's Centennial edition of *Leaves of Grass*. He even wrote to President Grover Cleveland, asking him to grant Whitman a government pension. Whitman eventually received patronage from Andrew Carnegie, who called him "the great poet of America so far."

Irish writer James Joyce, who was best known for his modernist novel *Ulysses* and his innovative stream of consciousness writing technique, was another popular writer of the Gilded Age. Joyce's life was that of a typical struggling artist, especially in the beginning. But he survived with his salary as an English teacher and financial support from his brother. Just when it appeared that his career as a writer would never get off the ground, he got a letter from a complete stranger. Well-known poet and critic Ezra Pound contacted Joyce after hearing about him and offered to try and help him sell his writing. He used his contacts to get the word out about Joyce and even published one of his poems in an anthology of poems. He connected him with everyone he could in the literary world and introduced him to what would become his greatest financial patron, Harriet Weaver. It was because of Weaver that Joyce was able to spend full-time on his writing. She set up Egoist Press to publish *A Portrait of the Artist as a Young Man* when it was turned down by other publishers. She had *Ulysses* printed outside the country when all other printers refused to print it due to its controversial nature.

After *Ulysses* was published, Joyce claimed he was too exhausted to write. It would be a whole year before he picked up a pen and started working on *Finnegan's Wake*, a work where Joyce took his stream of consciousness and free dream association to the limit. He veered off course from the normal plot and character style of a regular novel and wrote the book in his own, obscure language. It was *Finnegan's Wake* that caused Weaver to sever ties with the controversial writer she had given over a million dollars to over the years. Joyce received several private and public grants over his lifetime including the Civil List grant, Royal Literary Fund, and the Society of Authors. He also received patronage from some of his wealthy and generous students. Many of them paid for lessons they knew they would never receive.

Edgar Allen Poe was an unknown and struggling writer when he entered a literary contest sponsored by the Baltimore *Saturday Visitor*. His prose story "MS. Found in a Bottle" won the author fifty dollars and the admiration the judges who described Poe as "Distinguished by a vigorous and poetical imagination, a rich style, a fertile invention, and varied and curious learning."

Poe's initial years in Baltimore were extremely creative, though he was still living the life of a starving artist. In fact, much of his life was spent below the poverty level, even though he was a prolific and ingenious writer. But like Dickens, he became a public speaker and started earning a reputation as a super star on the circuit by both the critics and the public. His first speech was given at Philadelphia's William Wirt Institute to a sold out crowd. Critics said Poe had "great analytical power, command of language and strength of voice, and qualities which are rarely associated in a public speaker." They went on to say that Poe's performance was "second to none, if not superior to all lectures ever delivered before the Wirt Institute." Subsequent speeches earned him standing ovations and invitations to return.

Poe's speaking deeply touched his audiences and many said that once you heard his voice you could never forget it. He tended to recite his poetry in a unique sing-song manner that almost sounded like music. His life's struggles were seamlessly woven through his speeches and spoken through his colorful characters. Though Edgar Allen Poe was a genius, he didn't have the entrepreneurial business sense of writers like Shakespeare and Dickens, and he didn't have the patronage they had either. While Shakespeare and Dickens died very wealthy, Poe died penniless, mysteriously found in a ditch. The riddle surrounding his death would never be solved and only deepened the enigma of his life and creative talent.

A well-known writer of the twentieth-century, Langston Hughes, was a pioneer in black literature. He was a poet, novelist, and playwright who was best known as the leader of the Harlem Renaissance. He was quite prolific and wrote in any style he could to get his message across, including songs, biographies, histories, short stories, children's stories, and essays.

He was also an early innovator of a style known as jazz poetry. Hughes incorporated the repetitive phrases and syncopated rhythms of jazz and blues into his poetry. He wanted to distinguish his work from that of white poets. Jazz poetry could be said to be a precursor of modern rap and hip-hop music. It was adopted by the beat generation in the 1950s and eventually became a symbol of anti-establishment and counterculture movements. This carried over into the 60s with the hippie movement.

Hughes enjoyed a combination of patronage and an entrepreneurial spirit, along with his talent as a writer. He earned a bachelor's degree from Lincoln University through the assistance of patrons and would continue climbing in his career with the help of patronage, both public and private. It was after the publication of "The Weary Blues" that he met one of his most influential patrons, a wealthy woman named Charlotte Mason. Mason was supporting several writers during the Harlem Renaissance and requested that they call her "Godmother."

Mason gave Hughes $150 a month in financial aid so that he could focus his time and energy doing nothing else but writing. This also included his social life. In return she asked that she be consulted on his progress and that he provide her with a monthly itemized account of his expenses. Mason also gave him such perks as new suits and opera tickets. He would continue to be supported by patronage for two years so he was able to spend all of his time writing. One of the first projects to come out of this was his first novel *Not Without Laughter*, a semi-autobiographical account of his childhood growing up in the Midwest.

His patron "Godmother" had a profound influence on the style and content of the novel to the point of it being called censorship. It opens the door to a discussion on whether a financial patron should have the ability to censor an artist's work if they are paying that artist to create. *Not Without Laughter* would go on to win the Harmon Foundation Gold Award for literature and a $400 prize awarded to outstanding black artists. This spurred an increased interest in Hughes and a greater determination for him to make his living solely as a writer.

His next patronage would come from a Rosenwald Fund grant, which he used to tour black colleges in the South. He attracted a large following with his public speaking, even though his subject matter was often controversial. One wealthy patron of the arts, Noel Sullivan, had always wanted to be a singer but lacked the artistic ability. So instead he opened up his San Francisco mansion to artists he felt had the talent to become successful. He let Hughes stay in his luxurious mansion rent-free and had his housekeepers and cooks feed him and wait on him. They had lavish parties that included artists of all kinds. If this sounds familiar, it's exactly what happened in the Roman Era where artists lived in the homes of their patrons, ate their food, and mingled with their wealthy and influential friends. Besides winning the Rosenwald, he was also a Guggenheim fellow and won a grant from the American Academy of Arts and Letters. He left part of his legacy in the Harlem community by forming the Harlem Suitcase Theater, an experimental theater-in-the-round, whose mission was to promote interracial plays.

❧

As noted earlier, traveling shows of all kinds were making their way across America in the nineteenth century. Showmen, like John Durang, had to be versatile and play many parts in each show; he himself was an actor, singer, dancer, clown, puppeteer, and tightrope walker. He also worked behind the scenes and knew so much about the business that he eventually started his own company. Today the most successful entertainment entrepreneurs have both the business and the entertainment background.

Though George Clooney has big name recognition himself, he also runs his own production studio called Smokehouse Films. Brad Pitt is on the A list, but he also runs his own production company called Plan B. Will Smith had a successful music and acting career before starting his production company, Overbrook Entertainment. Queen Latifa also had a successful music and acting career before starting her company, Flavor Unit Entertainment.

Back in the 1800s, Edwin Booth, the second oldest son of well-known actor Junios Brutus Booth, became known as one of the most promising young actors in nineteenth-century America after his record-breaking 100 performances of Hamlet in New York City. He was also an entrepreneur, building his own venue, Booth's Theatre, which was both grand in scale and innovative in style. Though the movie industry would later disrupt commercial theater, and many small town commercial playhouses either closed or were converted into movie theaters, the movies never completely replaced live theater, and people still wanted to be entertained by both.

This is when small groups and associations started taking a lesson from the European Art Theater Movement. The groups produced local, community theater, which was called "Little Theater." The term "community theater" was eventually preferred, as the talent and themes were pooled from the resources of their communities and reflected their values. Philanthropists Alice and Irene Lewisohn built the Neighborhood Playhouse. They started it and funded it so they could experiment without being dependent on any outside funding. They had the freedom to fail.

As a young man, Otto Kahn had his heart set on being a poet and playwright, and he played various musical instruments. But his parents pushed him into the banking world. He went on to accumulate massive wealth as a banker, but he never gave up his love of art. It was because of his parent's condemnation of it that he was determined to become one of the world's most prolific art patrons. I guess Otto Kahn could be labeled a dilettante like Lorenzo do Medici, who was also a poet and liked to hang out with poets and artists.

Artists who called Kahn's office asking for financial help were told to write a letter listing their credentials, a mutual acquaintance who could validate their talent, and an explanation of how Kahn could help them. His patronage differed from Lorenzo's in that he preferred to make loans to artists instead of giving them grants. Just like art patronage back in the Roman Era, he would introduce his artists to influential people who could hire them. Then it was up to the artists to take it from there and prove themselves.

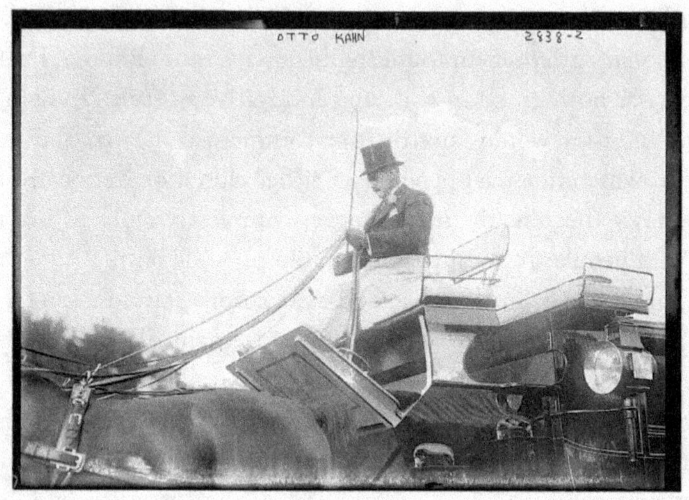

His patronage wasn't so much a personal relationship as it was a banker relationship. He didn't tell his artists what they could spend money on or what kind of art to produce but thought of it more as a breather for them so they could take time out and focus on their art without having to worry about finances. His patronage included the Metropolitan Opera, whose $500,000 debt was paid off. He also brought the Ballets Russes to America and financed struggling artists such as Herman Mankiewicz, Isadora Duncan, and Paul Robeson. He became one of the most influential art patrons in US history and was, in fact, known as "Otto the Magnificent," hearkening back to Lorenzo Medici.

You could say the female version of Otto Kahn was Alice Delamar, a goldmining heiress. She was a patron of art, ballet, and theater. When her father died she inherited $10 million dollars. She became a patron, and lover, to Eva Le Gallienne, a pioneer in the American Repertory Movement, a precursor to Off-Broadway. Not only was Le Gallienne a talented theater actor, but she was also an entrepreneur. Le Gallienne made her acting debut in London in 1914 after graduating from the Royal Academy of Dramatic Arts. After enjoying some success in the theater, she approached the Actor's Theatre, asking them to produce Ibsen's "The Master Builder" with her in the starring role. They turned her down. So she decided to mount the production herself and traveled around the country to enthusiastic audiences and glowing reviews.

Le Gallienne realized she could chart her own path and produce and star in her own productions. At the height of her fame she was twenty-seven and ready for a new challenge. With the financial backing of Otto Kahn and her lover Alice De Lamar she created the Civic Repertory Theatre, America's first classical repertory theater. In the late 1930s she co-founded the American Repertory Theatre with director Margaret Webster and producer Cheryl Crawford.

Lamar left Le Gallienne $1 million in her will, supporting her career as a patron for 60 years. Though she never had a family of her own, she had many friends, especially ones in the arts, and was generous and loyal to them. When her friend, architect Addison Mizner, was going through financial hardship, De Lamar helped him out financially and also commissioned journalist Ida Tarbell to write a book about him.

Another entrepreneurial theater patron was Lucille Lortel. Lortel started out as an actor but retired at the request of her wealthy husband, who was a paper industrialist and philanthropist. She then spent years trying to find an outlet for her creativity and talent that her husband would approve of. Since she could experiment without the pressure of having to make money, she converted an old horse barn on their property and called it The White Barn Theatre. The theater was established to be an escape from traditional theatrical commercial productions, which were expensive and didn't take any risks with experimental material.

Lortel wanted the White Barn to be a place where actors could stretch their talents, and writers could test out new and innovative works. She reveled in her role as a patron of the arts and was known to give gifts to those artists who praised her. She was also known to withhold money if someone displeased her. Her husband bought her a Manhattan theater for their 24th anniversary. The Lucille Lortel Theatre, as it's currently known, allows non-profit works to be staged there. This is in keeping with her idea that theater doesn't always need to be commercial, especially for experimental works. She continued her art patronage after her husband's death, establishing the Lucille Lortel Fund for New Drama at Yale University. The fund supports the production of new plays at the Yale Repertory Theatre. The Drama Circle Awards was another entity that she helped to fund, along with contributions to music and dance groups.

Another art patron of that time was Mary Bok, founder of the Curtis Institute of Music in Philadelphia. Bok was the only child of newspaper and magazine magnate, Cyrus Curtis and Louisa Knapp Curtis, founder of the *Ladies Home Journal*. Bok supported music students by giving a $150,000 donation to the Settlement Music School, and in 1924 she established the Curtis Institute of Music. She gave the school a $12 million endowment to help the musically gifted. She was a prolific philanthropist and genuine lover of the arts, who gave generously to artists, including her lifelong friend, actress Annie Russell. In 1930 she donated $100,000 to Rollins College to build a theater that Russell would control as its director.

Even before Mary Bok built the theater, Annie Russell herself was an entrepreneur. She formed her own theater company so she could pick and choose the roles she wanted to play. The public liked to see her typecast as a wilting violet. But she wanted to show her range as the strong woman she was. At the time it was very unusual for a woman to create and run her own theater company. Russell would become instrumental in the patronage of another fellow artist when she introduced Mary Bok to her friend Jules Andre Smith, who worked with Annie in a summer theater in Connecticut.

Jules Andre Smith was an architect and war artist for the United States Army during World War I. He put his architectural skills to good use designing sets for a local theater company. He had an entrepreneurial side and wrote a book called *The Scenewright: The Making of Stage Models and Settings*, which became a well-known resource in the craft of set design. Smith dreamed of building a retreat where fellow artists could create and develop new ideas without having to worry about the daily demands of life and how to pay the bills. In the 1930s he ended up in central Florida and decided to build a winter home and studio there. He loved the area, but one thing was missing… contemporary art.

Through Mary Bok's patronage he was able to purchase six acres of land and establish The Research Studio, which is now known as the Maitland Art Center in Maitland, Florida. In its heyday it was a winter residence of several prominent American artists. These artists became known as Bok fellows. The Research Studio was a thriving center for artists for over two decades under Smith's direction and Bok's patronage. He wrote two more books and spent his time at the retreat giving classes and putting on exhibitions. His beloved retreat is now a national historic landmark.

The Government as Patron of Arts and Entertainment

*"The Constitution only gives people the right to
pursue happiness. You have to catch it yourself."*

Benjamin Franklin

Government commissioned art has always been a part of history, and rulers have used it for thousands of years as a means to display their power or wealth. Julius Caesar, for one, liked to surround himself with the most distinguished writers he could find. They would write his speeches and create propaganda campaign materials, and in return, the writers would be given political favors, such as high ranking jobs in the military. This was true for visual arts as well, and the wealth of Roman art still enjoyed today bears witness to the power of public art.

Later, during the Reformation, Martin Luther became a master of art propaganda as both sides, Protestant and Catholic, constantly tried to make the other side look as bad as possible through printed material, songs, and visual artwork. And hundreds of years after that, Adolph Hitler would also exploit the power of art as propaganda. Hitler's original dream was to become an artist, but he failed the art academy's admission test twice. He spent his youth as a starving artist, often sleeping in the street and selling postcard drawings to tourists. Many of his early patrons, who bought his work and commissioned others, were Jews, and he sold most of his paintings to Jewish art dealers.[12]

Once Hitler got into power, he required all art to fit his standards. He then compiled a list of artists he deemed "divinely gifted." There were about 1,000 artists on the list and they were given special treatment. They paid fewer taxes, were exempt from military service, and, best of all, were "allowed" to work as artists, assuming they did their jobs as propaganda tools for the regime. Artists on the list were required to perform for soldiers and SS officers stationed at concentration camps. [13]

Hitler hired propaganda expert Joseph Goebbels and created the Reich Chamber of Culture, which oversaw theatre, music, literature, fine arts, radio, film and the press. Over 40,000 artists were approved by the government, but all were forced to join the Reich Chamber of Visual Arts. If an artist proved themselves "politically unreliable" they were expelled from the Chamber and no longer permitted to paint, teach, or exhibit. Art studios were visited by the Gestapo to ensure all artists were following state requirements for paintings. [14]

But visual arts are not the only art form effective for propaganda. In music, contrafacta is a technique that takes a well-known song or jingle and changes the words for propaganda purposes. It works in the same way that a popular advertising jingle works

---

12 See http://www.newyorker.com/magazine/2002/08/19/hitler-as-artist.

13 http://www.dw.com/en/

   hitlers-chosen-artists-walked-fine-line-between-art-and-politics/a-1051153

14 http://www.historylearningsite.co.uk/nazi-germany/art-in-nazi-germany/

because of its repetition. The words to the propagandized songs were then distributed to the public through printed brochures.

Though governments in Europe have been patronizing the arts for years, in the United States, government support for the arts has always been hotly debated. First was the debate over whether tax payer money should support the arts, and then who should get the support, and what the art should be about. It seems that the Revolutionary War was the only subject Congress could agree on, and even that turned into an argument over which part of the Revolution should be represented. Ultimately the first commission for government art went to John Trumbell, who received $32,000 for four paintings.

Trumbell, who had served in the military, believed that history should be preserved as a tool for learning and not just to be recorded. He felt that patriotic art was able to capture the moment and could live on as a vivid memory of the time. Not everyone agreed; when Trumbell finished, Representative William McCoy responded: "if the fine arts cannot thrive in this country without government jobs... let them fail." These paintings still reside in the rotunda of the Capital building. And if you happen to have a $2 bill, check to see his painting of the Declaration of Independence on the back.[15]

Government sponsorship of art was slow to get started, but once it got rolling, public arts projects grew in popularity. One of the first projects was the Smithsonian Institution, which wasn't even actually funded by the taxpayers, or even an American citizen. British scientist James Smithson inherited a sizable amount of money, which he left to his nephew. But in his will he specified that if his nephew died without any heirs, the money would go to the

---

15 Alan Howard Levy, *Government and the Arts: Debates over Federal Support of the Arts in America from George Washington to Jesse Helms,* Lantham, MD: University Press of America, 1997, 13.

US government to fund a site in Washington for the diffusion of knowledge. He also stipulated it was to be called the Smithsonian Institution. Though this seemed unlikely at the time, in a strange twist of fate, his nephew died just six years later in his twenties, leaving no heirs.

Luckily for the United States, Smithson left an endearing and lasting legacy, but he made no mention in his will of why he decided to leave it to the American people. It was never confirmed that he had ever even traveled to the States. Many have speculated about his reasons, but we may never know. Since a bequest like this had never been given before, Congress was at a loss as to exactly how to handle it. But they eventually passed legislation allowing President Andrew Jackson to accept the gift of $508,318.

The Smithsonian is now the world's largest museum complex, comprised of nineteen museums, four research centers, the National Zoo, a research library system, the *Smithsonian* magazine, and more. The institution is now funded through a combination of federal funding and donations from private sources, both corporate and individual. They also take in revenue from their magazine, restaurants, gift shops, online catalog, and concessions.

In the late 1800s, US cities were growing at a rapid pace, due to both a steady influx of immigrants and rural folks lured there by the expanding job market. By the early 1900s several of those cities already had over a million residents. But with this influx of people came other problems, like health and sanitation issues, pollution, overcrowding, and urban decay. The middle and upper-middle class would take advantage of what the city had to offer, like restaurants, theaters, and shopping, but afterwards they headed to their nice, comfortable homes outside the city limits in what would become the suburbs. It was the poor who were trapped in the cities, dealing with the slow decay around them.

This prompted an urban planning movement called the City Beautiful Movement. It was led by middle and upper middle class reformers, architects, and landscapers as a way to re-instill a sense of civic pride. Members of the City Beautiful Movement also felt beautification would lower the crime rate, which would help those living there as well as those who wanted to work and visit the city. So, civic pride was a good deal for everyone.

In the beginning the movement was concentrated in Washington D.C., Chicago, Detroit, and Cleveland but soon spread across the country. The plans included monuments, parks, and community gardens. The City Beautiful Movement led to the creation of other art societies such as The Municipal Art Society, who promoted the idea that art could benefit the public. [16]

The City Beautiful Movement also inspired the establishment of the U.S. Commission of Fine Arts in 1910. It was an advisory board that could help guide and advise the federal government on art, architecture, landscaping, and urban design. It weighed in on design for government buildings, coins, medals, and memorials and supported the development of art institutions.

Following the stock market crash of 1929, the unemployment rate skyrocketed to 25 percent. By 1932, over 13 million Americans had lost their jobs, and the average household income had dropped by 40 percent. As a result, FDR established the Works Progress Administration as a way to put Americans back to work. Several arts related projects were formed under the WPA, which became known collectively as Federal Project Number One.

One of these was the Federal Writers Project, and at its peak it employed 6600 writers, editors, historians, teachers, librarians, and researchers. The original purpose of this project was to write and produce a series of guide books called the American Guide Series. Intended to shine a light on America's historical, scenic, cultural,

---

16 Gregory Gilmartin, *Shaping the City: New York and the Municipal Art Society* see "Shaping the City: New York and the Municipal Art Society, Clarkson Potter Publishers, 1995.

and economic resources, the Writers Project soon expanded to include other projects like city guides and regional and cultural guides. The publications included books, articles, brochures, speeches, and radio scripts.

Though the project did accomplish the goal of putting writers to work, it wasn't exactly the kind of work writers had envisioned. The hours were 8 am until 5 pm and paid between $20-$25 a week. Many of the writers were actually embarrassed by the publications they put out and were depressed by the tediousness of the work, which at the time didn't seem to make a difference, and lacked the freedom of creativity they were hoping for. But the work of the Writers Project has proven to be a valuable chronicle of American history and culture and is housed in the Library of Congress.

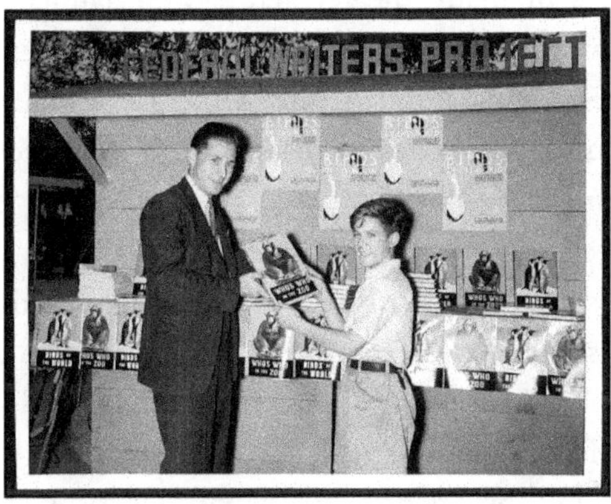

The Federal Arts Project was formed to fund the visual arts. It was the largest of the New Deal projects and lasted from 1935 to 1943. Unlike previously government-funded art that relied on hiring the best artists to capture US history in paintings, the Federal Arts Project provided employment to out of work painters, designers, and sculptors, regardless of whether they were the best artists or not. Like New Deal writers, artists were paid as day laborers. In essence, the American tax payers were their patrons. Writer and Arts administrator Edgar Holger Cahill became the national director. His goal was to make art accessible to the common man. Under his direction, community art centers sprang up in cities and towns across the country, employing over 10,000 artists and crafts workers.

The Federal Theatre Project was another ambitious undertaking by the federal government to put unemployed actors, directors, playwrights, and stage technicians and designers back to work. It was created by FDR in 1935 and lasted until funding ran out in 1939. Besides putting unemployed theater people back to work, the Federal Theatre Project was also hoping to revitalize theater in general and make it accessible for the millions of Americans who had never seen live theater. It did accomplish that goal, as the productions were seen by over 30 million people nationwide in over 200 theaters in 40 states.

The careers of many theater actors were launched under the Federal Theatre Project, including Orson Welles, Martin Ritt, Elia Kazan, John Houseman, and Arthur Miller. Houseman and Welles would strike up a collaboration that lasted through to the production of *Citizen Kane*.

The project was spearheaded by Hallie Flanagan Davis, a university professor, producer, director, playwright and author. She incorporated some of the experimental concepts she learned while traveling around Europe and was the first woman to receive a Guggenheim Fellowship to study theater there.[17]

Three previous presidents—Buchanan, Harrison, and Theodore Roosevelt—had tried and failed to establish a national council on the arts. FDR's WPA was the first, followed by Lyndon B. Johnson establishing the National Endowment for the Arts and the National Endowment for the Humanities in 1965. The NEA's purpose was to offer funding and support for projects that exhibited artistic excellence and "foster the excellence, diversity, and vitality of the arts in

---

17 Edwin Wilson and Alan Goldfarb, *Living Theater*, McGraw-Hill Book Company, 1983, 311-12.

the United States." To determine that excellence, the NEA chairperson chose a panel to decide. Panel members were required to have expertise in the kind of art they would be judging.

The NEA program wasn't meant to fully subsidize the arts in the United States but to offer seed money so that the private sector could grow the arts. It was meant to preserve the arts historically and foster new artistic growth. The arts that are included under the NEA include:

- Dance
- Drama
- Music
- Painting
- Sculpture
- Photography
- Creative writing
- Graphic art
- Motion pictures
- Television
- Radio
- Costume
- Fashion design
- Crafts
- Architecture
- Sound recordings

Most funding grants go to large non-profit organizations with only a small amount going to individual artists. Those individual artists are usually ones who are already well known and distinguished in their fields, not beginners. Part of the reason the money goes to large art organizations and not individual artists is because it's easier to spread the funding around by targeting the biggest amount of artists possible at one time. It's also easier to spread it out geographically and include more racial, ethnic, and gender diversity.

It's also less of a risk of having an individual, unknown artist produce a piece of work that most people would find offensive.

Besides the NEA, government funding also includes state and local arts councils. Groups and programs supported by state arts boards and councils include:

- Artist residencies
- Public art
- Schools
- Individual artists
- Arts organizations
- Apprenticeships
- Cultural & heritage organizations

According to the NEA website, here is what they do and do not fund:

They DO fund:

- Projects that consist of one or more specific events or activities. These can be part of a regular season or activity. Organizations can undertake a single short-term project—a ten-day jazz festival, for example—or they could identify certain components (such as a key artist presentation and associated activities).
- Organizations for any or all phases of a project, from planning through implementation.
- Projects that are not new as they believe there can be excellent existing projects as well as new activities.
- Projects that are not large. The NEA notes it welcomes small projects that can make a difference in a community or field.
- All sorts of artist residencies that allow artists needed time and space to focus on their craft, from a few weeks to years. There are over 500 residencies in the United States and over

1500 worldwide with 90 percent of these programs involving local communities.

They DO NOT fund:

- General operating expenses or seasonal support or costs for creating new organizations.
- Direct grants to individuals—the NEA encourages applicant organizations to involve individual artists.
- Individual elementary or secondary schools directly, though schools may participate as project partners with eligible organizations such as local education agencies, school districts, and state and regional education agencies.
- Any construction, purchase, or renovation of facilities though design fees, exhibition space preparation, community planning, and the installation or de-installation of an artwork are covered.
- Any for-profit or commercial enterprises or activities, such as concessions, food, T-shirts, etc.
- Compensation to foreign nationals and/or foreign travel or any visa expenses.
- Costs to bring a project into compliance with federal grant requirements including environmental or historical assessments. Also they do not fund any subgranting or regranting, except for state arts agencies, regional arts organizations, or local arts agencies that are designated to operate on behalf of their local governments
- Awards to individuals or organizations to honor or recognize achievement.
- Professional training programs or projects that replace arts instruction provided by an arts specialist.
- Any publishing that does not focus on contemporary literature and/or writers and any publication of books or

exhibition of works by the applicant organization's board members, faculty, or trustees.

- Single, individually-owned exhibitions and any projects that are based on criteria other than artistic excellence and merit, such as festivals or exhibitions.
- Project costs supported by any other federal funding.
- Social activities (such as receptions, parties, galas), alcoholic beverages, gifts and prizes, contributions and donations to other entities.
- Lobbying, endowments, marketing expenses that are not directly related to the project, most audit costs, fines and penalties, bad debt costs, deficit reduction, or rental costs for home office workspace.

Art residencies can be nice opportunities for upcoming and established artists. Some are working retreats that provide a quiet place to create without any distractions and some are placement as a guest artist within a community. Some residencies are fully funded or partially funded, and some you have to pay to attend. Some are prestigious invitation only for mostly established artists and some are for the total beginner. They are funded by government, individuals, corporations and private foundations.

Art residencies are about the creative process and not the final product. It's a place to experiment with your craft without being judged. It's where a new idea that may or may not be commercial has a chance to grow or fail on its own merits. The majority of art residencies are located in rural locations like remote cabins or isolated bungalows in the desert, where an artist can work and not be distracted. But it can also be a time for networking and building valuable relationships in addition to being inspired by other artists.

One of the more unusual residencies is a tiny tree house called Outlandia at the foot of Ben Nevis Mountain in the Scottish Highlands. Artists are encouraged to integrate nature and natural resources into their proposals. The awe-inspiring space makes it easy to unplug from the world and concentrate on simply creating good art. The Antarctic Artists and Writers Program is sponsored by the National Science Foundation. They are looking for artists who share their mission to increase appreciation for scientific research and education. This is a program that includes round-trip airfare from the United States to the Southern Hemisphere but doesn't include salaries or materials.

I believe in an "all of the above" approach to sponsorship and patronage. Just like the early Renaissance artists, try every angle possible to get patronage, whether it's from corporations, small businesses, the public, foundations or from the government. Try it all!

And Now a Word From Our Sponsor

Corporate Sponsorship

*"A business that makes nothing but money
is a poor kind of business"*

Henry Ford

ART AND COMMERCE have been intertwined for decades. There has always been a debate about whether advertising qualifies as art or not. Both advertising and art are meant to move people, though it could be said that advertising is designed to move people to pull out their wallets and spend money, whereas art doesn't. Creators of advertising and art are both paid, but sometimes artists create art to feed their souls. Advertising isn't created for the same purpose.

Art can be interpreted differently by different people. One person's idea of a great painting or song might be offensive to someone else. Advertising is meant to be more definitive. The purpose of an ad should be pretty clear, although some ads make you wonder what they are even selling.

According to John F. Perriss, Chairman of the Global Media Commission International Advertising Agency, "whether it is used to promote a company, a product or a service, sponsorship can achieve results that advertising cannot, due to third party participation, and the focused attention of the target group. It therefore complements advertising and, when well conceived and executed, is created and carried out with the same thorough professionalism as advertising."[18]

The lines between charity and commercial sponsorship are blurry, and many people don't know the difference. When asked about sponsorship, people often say "We've already given to charity this year." This confusion is easy to understand as sponsorship still has an air of mystery to it. It doesn't always fit neatly into a box. Philanthropy, patronage, marketing, and advertising seem to overlap in many cases. A good rule of thumb, if you want to determine whether something is charity or a commercial venture, is if you would be willing to give your money anonymously without getting anything in return for it.

The most striking example of art as commerce is the work of Andy Warhol. Before he achieved fame as a pop artist in museum circles, he was a very successful consumer ad designer. He also used his artistic talent to design album covers and promotional materials. He was the first artist to take something as simple and commercial as a Campbell Soup can and turn it into a piece that ended up in a museum. So, would you call this advertising or art? It really depends on where the soup can is.

If the soup can is in the marketing department of Campbell's Soup or on a billboard, it's advertising. If it's next to a Rembrandt in the museum, it's art. What Warhol did do was to get us to look at the world and art in a different way. His art has been purchased for the offices of corporations like Progressive Insurance and J. P. Morgan Chase. Warhol prints were commissioned by the Phillip

---

18 Global Media Commission of the International Advertising Agency. *Sponsorship: It's Role and Effects,* New York, NY: International Advertising Agency, 1988, 1.

Morris tobacco company for a traveling exhibition. They had the first national ad campaign to let the public know about the traveling exhibition they were sponsoring.

One reason sponsorship and advertising seem to overlap is because we've always talked about TV and radio as having sponsors. The announcer would always say "And now a word from our sponsor…" TV and radio both resisted commercial interference and tried to stick to educational programming that would benefit the public. The public also resisted the idea of direct advertising but eventually gave in to the idea of indirect advertising as the price they would have to pay for good programming.

For example, "An association of greeting card manufacturers sponsored a talk on the history of Christmas cards. Gillette provided a discourse on fashions in beards since medieval times, culminating in the triumph of the safety razor."[19] This was constantly a work in progress as executives had to decide what was appropriate to put on the air and how much a sponsor could get away with. It was always a battle to decide who got to go how far. A manufacturer of vitamins was told they couldn't have commercials running during kids programming, but the manufacturers of sweet, sugary breakfast cereals could. In the beginning, no prices could be mentioned, no free samples, and no mention of where the product could be bought. What a change that is from today's infomercial!

In the early 1920s, commercial radio stations started broadcasting in the United States and used sustaining programs, or programming on a commercial station that didn't use commercial sponsorship. Instead of paid advertising, programming was paid for from the sale of radio equipment, since the patented equipment manufacturers established most of the radio stations. The rest were operated by universities for educational purposes and funded

---

19 Erik Barnouw, *The Sponsor: Notes on a Modern Potentate,* New York, NY: Transaction, 1978, 16-17.

through endowments and some city governments for public benefit. Additionally, in rural areas, the US Department of Agriculture produced such programming as weather forecasts, household hints, and market reports.[20]

As more and more people owned radios the medium progressed and began to hit a critical mass. Programs were becoming more polished, requiring more money to produce. The idea of taxing radio was quickly shot down for fear of a complete government takeover of the airwaves. Besides, listeners were already used to getting their radio programming for free and didn't want to have to pay for it. But something had to change if the quality was going to be kept up and the programming was going to be free to listen to. So sponsorship from companies became a viable solution, and the radio industry put out an aggressive campaign to promote it.

As radio became national and centralized, big corporate sponsors took over and started controlling the programming. Just like big corporate sponsorship today, it was about how many listeners you could get. The more listeners heard about a product or company, the better the return on investment. Sponsorship, even socially responsible sponsorship, helps to improve the bottom line.

Before the Nielsen ratings came along to determine radio listener data, radio programmers were in the dark as far as who was listening and what they wanted to hear, clearly valuable information for sponsors. So, early radio announcers sent out notices to listeners to determine demographics and what the listeners wanted to hear on the program. They found out that people didn't mind sponsorship (as long as it wasn't overdone) because they got better quality programming with more professional talent.

By the late 1920s to early 1930s, the sponsored musical feature, with naming rights, became a popular radio format, such as the

---

20 Susan Smulyan, *Selling Radio: The Commercialization of American Broadcasting 1920-1934*, Washington, DC: Smithsonian, 1996, 67.

Champion Spark Plug Hour, The A & P Gypsies, and King Biscuit Time. Classical music programs included The Bell Telephone Hour and The Voice of Firestone. Metropolitan Opera radio broadcasts were sponsored by Texaco and are still broadcast to this day by the Toll Brothers. This is similar to modern day sponsorship where a corporation or organization will claim the naming rights to an event or a college stadium.

This was a perfect solution to otherwise distracting advertising and is primarily how sponsorship of arts and education works today. Sponsorship is meant to be non-intrusive. Commercials would be considered an interference, but sponsorship is much more subtle and doesn't detract from enjoyment of the program.

As sponsorship changed, programs began to change. "Broadcasters considered programming as something for listeners to hear when they turned on the radio, while advertising professionals needed to think about what programs might make listeners *want* to turn on the radio."[21] Just like sponsorship today, it was all about how many people were listening to or watching the program being sponsored. So, it became the responsibility of the sponsor and the broadcaster to promote whatever program was being sponsored to as many people as possible.

They promoted the *program*, not the *product*. This is why sponsorship is called a partnership. Artists and educators need to promote events as much as the sponsor and should use every promotional tool possible to maximize their sponsor's investment. Both parties were encouraged to promote the program in a wide variety of different media, like newspapers, magazines, trade papers, direct mail, outdoor displays, and automobile advertising. All of these methods can and should be used today, along with TV and other publicity channels.

The one sponsor format changed again to become what we now

---

21 Ibid, 83

have, which is multiple sponsorships, for programming. It all happened thanks to a woman known as "The Nation's Homemaker," Ida Bailey Allen. Allen started out as the food editor for a local daily newspaper, and in 1928 she started hosting a regular daytime radio show. She also produced the show, and like many radio hosts today, she sold her own advertising. Being a naming sponsor for the whole show was rather expensive. So, she decided to sell individual spots for sponsors who wanted to support the show but couldn't afford to take on the financial responsibility of the whole program. The sponsors were integrated into the show, as she made her recipes using the sponsor's products.

This is how I see small business sponsorship as the future for arts and education. Small businesses are shut out of the major sporting events, like the Olympics or a major league baseball team. The opportunities for artists and speakers to partner with small businesses are endless. And having multiple sponsors is an even more viable solution for both. Artists and speakers will make more money, and small business sponsors will share the expense of sponsorship. Like Ida's show, there are plenty of ways to integrate your sponsor into your work without making it look like a paid commercial.

Ida Bailey Allen was a prolific writer and penned fifty cookbooks. She was also smart at partnering with corporations and wrote a promotional book for Coca Cola called "When You Entertain," which sold over 375,000 copies in less than 6 months. During World War II, she became a speaker for the US Food Administrator and a popular speaker on the lecture circuit at places like the Women's Book Club. If you happened to live in or visit New York City, you could set up an appointment to watch Ida live in her kitchen.

Today it's common for podcast hosts to also have their own newsletter that they send out to their audience. But Ida was a pioneer in that kind of marketing, realizing the enormous potential she had as a radio host to reach a lot of people and sell far more books.

Her audience members received a membership card and could win prizes for the best recipes.

Once television came along, sponsors dropped radio for the shiny, new medium that was more visually appealing. Radio was expected to replace newspapers, but that never happened. And television was expected to replace radio, which also never happened. Both simply innovated and found other audiences. Radio sponsorship had set the template for TV and it stayed the same.

TV programming, like radio programming, started out with single sponsorship, such as The Texas Star Theater, hosted by Milton Berle. Other shows included "Kraft Television Theater," which had the highest sponsor identification of any show on TV in the late 1940s. "Robert Montgomery Presents" was another live drama show that had several sponsors during the seven years it was on air. The show title changed whenever the sponsor changed, like "Robert Montgomery Presents Your Lucky Strike Theater" or "Robert Montgomery Presents the Johnson's Wax Program." This was a way to customize sponsorship, which is going to become even more important in all media in the future.

Slowly TV sponsorship began to change. For one thing it was becoming too expensive for a single sponsor to carry the weight of a whole one-hour show. Shows that were cheap to produce, like game shows, became popular until the discovery that single sponsors were rigging the game shows and letting popular contestants win. Shows were originally produced and broadcast live from New York before pre-recorded shows moved to Hollywood in the mid 1950s. In a few years, network shows would become a combination of filmed, taped, and live broadcast. TV networks took over production from the sponsors.

Fine art has also been "sponsored" for centuries. The first corporate fine art collection was formed in 1472 by Monte dei Paschi bank during the Renaissance. The first corporate art sponsorship in the U.S. started in the 1940s and was funded mostly by privately owned manufacturing companies and banks. But today a wide variety of industries sponsor artists of all kinds.

In the 1950s and 60s American art became more important internationally as corporate growth increased dramatically. Most corporate fine art collections started after 1960, and corporations used them as a competitive advantage. Corporations also began to commission artists to create sculptures and paintings for their corporate headquarters, host artists in residence, sponsor music, theater and dance companies, and put on museum exhibits.[22]

David Rockefeller, former Chairman of the Chase Manhattan Bank and Founder of the Business Committee for the Arts, once said "I think of art as the highest level of creativity. To me, it is one of the greatest sources of enjoyment." Rockefeller believed that corporations had an obligation to have a greater financial involvement in the patronage of the arts and that they could do that without losing sight of the need to make a profit. In 1966 Rockefeller gave a speech entitled "Culture and the Corporation" where he brought prominent business leaders together for the purpose of forming an organization called the Business Committee for the Arts to promote a partnership between the business community and artists. The organization was to have "certain standards of good citizenship."

In his speech he said "I feel it would be enormously helpful for representatives of business and the arts to exchange views face to face, to seek new ideas from each other, to clarify misunderstandings and explore new possibilities." The Business Committee for the Arts was officially launched in 1967. Rockefeller came up with four ways to broaden the base of corporate support:

1. Conduct research to find out which corporations are already voluntarily supporting the arts

2. Provide counseling to corporations who are interested in supporting the arts

------

22 Martorella, *Art and Business,* 1

3. Supply information to corporations so they could be aware of the types of opportunities that exist in the arts and let them know what others are doing to support the arts

4. Help arts organizations obtain support from corporations

The government encourages support from the private sector by offering tax incentives to help offset budget cutbacks. In a good economy, corporations tend to increase their artist commissions, fine art collecting, and sponsorship of museum exhibits, art galleries, and live performing arts events. A public-private sector art collaboration is good for the economic impact of industrial cities. The tourism industry alone is a multi-billion dollar industry.

According to the Foundation Center, the world's leading source of information on philanthropy, fundraising, and grant programs, big corporations prefer to sponsor things like big budget, well-known performing arts projects and high profile museum exhibits because they can get more exposure from them. Arts organizations need to prove to the sponsor that their event will enhance the corporation's public image, increase their visibility, and improve their bottom line. It's also easier to justify their investment in the sponsorship if the event is high profile.

Michael Kaiser, Chairman of Devos Institute of Arts Management, has noticed a radical change in the way big corporations sponsor the arts. In a recent Huffington Post article he said, "Good will has been replaced by business objectives. It's hard work to receive a major corporate gift in today's environment. They want profits that turn into higher share prices." That doesn't mean it's impossible for today's artist or small local arts organizations to get corporate funding, it just means today's artist must learn how to collaborate with businesses and become an entrepreneurial partner.[23]

Artists need to have some knowledge about how business works

---

23   https://www.huffingtonpost.com/michael-kaiser/corporate-support-for-the_b_853148.html

and how they can help them improve their bottom line. It's not enough these days for most artists to just be a great talent. Unless you're on the A list, you need to be business savvy and help a corporation bring in a good ROI. According to a *New York Times* article written by Robin Pogrebin, "When companies do support culture, they are increasingly paying for it out of their marketing budgets, which means strings are attached to the funds: from how a corporation's name will appear in promotional materials, to what parties it can give during an exhibition, to the number of free or discounted tickets available to its employees."

The better the economy is doing and the better a corporation is doing financially, the more they will contribute to the arts. Even when the economy isn't doing that well, corporations will still keep up some of their corporate sponsorship because it's simply a good business practice. And it's not just big corporations that are sponsoring artists. Small businesses are starting to get in on it also. In fact, as corporate sponsorship has gotten more difficult to obtain, small businesses are seeing it as a chance to experiment with new marketing techniques instead of simply advertising. They see the opportunities to get their products, their services, and their brands in front of a targeted audience by partnering with the art community.

A recent study by the Indiana University Center on Philanthropy showed that small businesses in Indiana consistently give at least 3 percent of their net income to charity as opposed to 1-2½ percent from large corporations. This proves what I have always believed to be true, that small business arts and education sponsorship is a gold mine waiting to happen.

Small businesses have always been overlooked in favor of big corporations with deep pockets. But that is slowly changing as artists are learning how to be producers of their own creative projects. Access to small business is a much easier and faster road than waiting in line with hundreds of thousands of other artists for a chance to be sponsored by the likes of an IBM, NIKE, or Coca Cola. The perception of small businesses that they don't have enough money to sponsor artists is a myth. Small business art sponsorship can often be more than a large corporate sponsorship. My first small business sponsorship was over $60,000 for the production of a play in Los Angeles for a six-week run. Today that sponsorship would be worth even more.

Smart Growth America has put out a guide book called "(Re) Building Downtown: A Guidebook for Revitalization" aimed at those elected officials who wish to reinvigorate neighborhoods and promote economy and culture through a smart growth approach. Part of this plan details getting small local businesses involved by having them sponsor performing arts and fine arts festivals high-lighting local artists. Another part of the plan outlines permanent cultural facilities like museums, performing arts centers, historic sites, and other attractions to drive traffic to downtown areas.

Every year in Colorado Springs, local businesses sponsor the Trees of Life celebration, which honors the military and local community protectors by decorating trees with lights. The Pike's Peak Hospice Foundation puts this on in collaboration with the Downtown Partnership of Colorado Springs, with an in-kind dona-tion of space by the Colorado Springs Pioneers Museum. Pride, Inc. of Bismarck, North Dakota, puts on a similar event called the Celebration of Trees, which partners with local businesses who sponsor trees. The money is donated to an organization that helps integrate the disabled into the community so that they can live independent lives. After the event is over, the trees are donated to families who can't afford a Christmas tree.

The businesses aren't sponsoring because they expect to get immediate sales out of it but are doing it to align themselves with a good cause and promoting good will in the community. In other words, like the businesses sponsoring the Trees of Life celebration, they're building up good karma in the hopes that they will gain customers who like businesses who give back to a good cause and support the community. Research shows that most people want to buy from socially responsible businesses and ones that support their local communities.

Dialogue Brewing was started by four business partners just north of downtown Albuquerque, New Mexico. Two of the partners, Daniel Goreman and Ian LeBlanc, both came from the art world and wanted to incorporate art into their business so visitors could enjoy the scenery as they sipped on a cold beer. They wanted to promote art, and they did that with the installation of a unique sculpture garden of six steel trees.

Small businesses in brick and mortar locations have to compete with online stores and big box stores for customers. So it's even more important that they be able to drive traffic by being a destination or gathering place. They have to provide something the others don't have. One way is through experiential, grassroots marketing. In other words, give them an experience.

Amy's Ice Cream, with fifteen locations in Texas, knew that they had competition from big ice cream companies who could afford expensive TV advertising. So from the beginning they knew they had to be different. In the hiring process Amy accidentally stumbled on a way to hire creative employees. One day after running out of applications she gave out a plain, white paper bag and asked the potential employee to go home and decorate it. This turned into a unique hiring process that has yielded very creative people who have generated new and unique marketing ideas for the company.

One of those ideas came about when her employees started doing tricks with the ice cream to the amusement of customers waiting in line. This eventually turned into a local event called the Trick Olympics. Employees do the craziest stunts with ice cream while a DJ plays in the background. They also have a raffle and give donations to local charities.

Another great example of a small business community arts partnership is located in Framingham, Massachusetts. This innovative arts incubator, called Fire Seed Arts, literally started out with nothing and ended up creating jobs in the community, and are doing their part to save the planet at the same time. Founders Daniel Balter and Patino Vazquez shared a common interest in finding ways that trash could be transformed into beautiful pieces of art. They came up with the idea to start an eco lab at a local garbage dump. They decided that all of their materials would come from the garbage. Of course, they had to get permission from the city to do it, which they got.

Their mission was to create a bridge between local artists and the small business community. They took their first recycled artwork around to local businesses looking for sponsors. They started with a single, local restaurant, Viva Mexican Grill. Viva put their repurposed artwork on display in their restaurant. They've since gotten sponsors such as Tile Showcase, EMS Sports, and Whole Foods. They've expanded beyond just making art. They now have a band called Fire Seed Johnny and the Junkyard Dogs that uses instruments made entirely from materials they found in the trash. They sell Seed Ds of the music, teach art classes, and even rent out their newly decorated eco lab for events.

The community benefits from the art and music, the local artists get paid, and the small businesses get exposure for their business by sponsoring concerts and artwork, and by showing the community they support local artists who care about the environment. If you think you can't make a living as an artist when you have absolutely nothing, remember Fire Seed Arts and figure out how you can be creative from scratch and make the most of everything you have.

One reason companies will sponsor an event is so they will have a way to mingle with clients in a social atmosphere while entertaining them, educating them, or both. Carnegie Hall actively lists on their website the many perks corporate sponsors get when they become a patron. These include complimentary tickets, behind the scenes tours of the facilities, advance invitations and priority seating for gala benefits, company listing in Playbill all season, half price tickets for employees, exclusive access to dress rehearsal performances, VIP access for executives to their private lounge, and rent free access to banquet spaces. They will also create a special sponsorship package customized to suit your needs.

A large corporation may hire an art consultant or administrator with experience and contacts in the community who teams up with the CEO to put together a high quality art collection that reflects their brand. Many Fortune 500 CEOs are on boards at museums and performance arts organizations. Part of a corporate art administrator's job is to maintain the art, write brochures, create tours of artist's workshops, and create educational programs to educate employees about the art they purchase for the corporation. Corporate art tends to be non-controversial and pleasing to a wide group of people. A corporation's art collection tends to reflect their corporate brand and establishes their public image and corporate identity.

A smaller corporation with a lower budget might hire a decorator or consultant to purchase less expensive prints and works from local, unknown artists. Most corporate art is bought for decoration and not as an investment. In the beginning, corporations began funding the arts because of tax breaks. Though once they may have wanted it to be kept anonymous for fear of being overwhelmed by artists seeking funding, but today corporations want to be more visible when it comes to sponsoring artists, even though they are still overwhelmed by artists seeking sponsorship.

Corporate sponsorship is now seen as a way to improve your brand image by demonstrating your commitment to the community and your sense of corporate social responsibility. Corporations want the positive publicity that comes with it and choose to flaunt that image as much as possible. This is one reason corporations prefer to sponsor well established performing arts organizations who have an appeal to a wide audience and are capable of attracting higher visibility.

Another reason big corporations will sponsor arts and education is because of the political clout it brings them. For example, when a proposal was introduced in New York City to restrict smoking in public places, cigarette company Phillip Morris called all of the New York arts organizations they had given millions of dollars to and asked them to call their council members and oppose the measure. Not wanting to risk the withdrawal of their much needed funds, they complied.

Corporate social responsibility is voluntary. And tax benefits and good publicity aren't the only reasons corporations sponsor the arts. Big corporations today collect fine art as a capital asset and must explain and justify their art investment to the stockholders. The more valuable the collection, the more it costs to keep it up, with insurance, security and preservation.

Approximately one third of corporations sponsor local artists. Corporations prefer to hang local or regional art in their offices because it shows a commitment to the community, and it's also more affordable. They will purchase art from younger or less established artists as an investment and sell them later for a nice profit when the artist has become established. Corporations tend to sponsor artists who are popular in the communities where they have their headquarters. This opens the door for local and regional artists who are looking for big corporate sponsors but don't have national recognition yet.

This is a good reason for artists to start out with local and regional small business sponsors because it allows them to work on their craft as a paid artist while building up a name for themselves and a fan base in the city or region where the corporation has their headquarters. This gives the beginning or less established artist an edge over their competition. Big corporations and government don't tend to sponsor unknown performing artists. But, like the fine artist, if they start out with small business, local, and regional sponsorship and build up a name, that will attract the attention of a bigger corporation.

Regional art sponsorship is good for human resources because it attracts better talent. It provides a pleasant setting for entertaining high-end clients and boosts employee morale by enabling employees to communicate better with each other. Employees report more job satisfaction when they are surrounded by art. It tends to give the workplace a more humanizing environment. Corporate art helps stimulate employee's imaginations and creativity. The Progressive auto insurance company views their vast art collection as more of a cultural investment than a financial investment.

Big and small corporations love to commission original work from new, emerging, local and unknown artists. This helps to promote regional art and the culture of the community, which is a part of their corporate social responsibility. Buying local or regional art helps to promote regional styles of art. Sponsoring artists is good for the economy, and a strong economy means more working artists.

Private Foundations
& Grants

"Think of giving not only as a duty but as a privilege."

John Rockefeller

An important piece of the patronage partnership is grants. Philanthropists want to improve the human condition and make a positive change to society through their contributions. They are always looking for new and unique ways to improve their communities. Socrates said that the act of his giving away his thoughts in a speech was his philanthropy, and Plato left his farm to a nephew with instructions to use the profits from the harvest to help the students and teachers at the school he started.

Philanthropy in general, as we know it today, reached its peak in the Age of Enlightenment, when the act of doing good deeds to help your fellow human became a way of living a fulfilling and satisfying life. The first charitable organization to be incorporated was started by Captain Thomas Coram. After living in America for most of his life, he returned to his birthplace in England and was shocked to find the number of babies and young children who were left in the streets to die. At the time, mothers of illegitimate children were treated harshly by society. Captain Coram felt compelled to do something about it, but knew he couldn't do it alone. So he petitioned to obtain a Royal Charter from the king to start a hospital for exposed and abandoned children.

Almost twenty years later, the charter for the first Foundling Hospital was granted. It started with humble beginnings, but with the help of patronage it quickly grew. Just like in the history of art patronage, hospitals in the past were supported by either the church or the state. But the advent of a new type of hospital organization paved the way for artists to partner with non-profits that continues today.

One of Coram's artist friends, William Hogarth, donated a portrait he had painted of Coram to the hospital and encouraged other artists to follow his lead. This became London's first art gallery. In return, the artists that donated their paintings were made governors of the hospital. It's possible that the idea for the Royal Academy grew out of the meetings of the governors. It wasn't just fine artists who donated their work. Handel gave concerts in the chapel to raise money for the hospital.

To this day, art patronage and philanthropy continue at that institution. Even today, nonprofits and hospitals are partnering with artists to bring joy and healing to patients. RxArt was one of those nonprofits that was started by a patient, Diane Brown. Brown was working in cancer research while pursuing a masters in art history. It was her own experience in a hospital that sparked the idea for RX Art. While getting a CAT scan, she imagined a beautiful painting and it calmed her down. It was then that she knew she had to spread her love of art to as many hospitals as possible. Artists such as Keith Haring and Jeff Koons have worked with RxArt.

Fine art isn't the only kind of art that helps patients heal. Musicians on Call was created as a nonprofit to bring the healing power of live music to the bedsides of patients who need it most. Like fine art, music has the power to calm and improve blood pressure, emotional outlook, and pain tolerance. Musicians on Call has received celebrity support from artists such as Jewel, Jon Bon Jovi, Tim McGraw, and Justin Bieber.

In colonial times in America, the Massachusetts Bay Company chartered a board whose thirteen men were chosen to manage the colonial government. There would soon be an unwritten obligation for the rich in the community to take care of the poor, while the poor were obligated to do the best that they could. When Harvard University had its first fund raising, volunteers claimed they were "begging." But it turns out that their fund raising was quite a success, and that same year they created their first scholarship fund.

In 1889, Andrew Carnegie wrote an article called "The Gospel of Wealth" and called for industrialists to accumulate wealth and distribute it to benevolent causes. He believed that traditional charity didn't solve the real problems of poverty. Carnegie and John D. Rockefeller had both accumulated massive amounts of wealth on a scale that was unheard outside of royalty. Both men gave away most of their wealth to charity before they died. The Carnegie Foundation and the Rockefeller Foundation were both innovative in their large scale private philanthropy and funded museums, libraries, and educational institutions, among other things.

In 1922, Philadelphia physician and entrepreneur Alfred C. Barnes established The Barnes Foundation to promote arts education and appreciation. The story of the Barnes Foundation and his legacy, which includes art worth billions of dollars is the basis of a wonderful documentary called *The Art of the Steal*. When Barnes died in 1951, he left strict instructions on how his art was to be handled. But because he didn't have any heirs at the time, the foundation was left in the hands of loyal board members until they all passed away and there was a battle to save the Barnes legacy and the art he left to the public.

The Folger Shakespeare Library in Washington, DC, is home to the world's largest Shakespeare collection and other rare books and works of art from the Renaissance. It was donated to the American people by the Folger family. Henry Folger, former president and chairman of the board of Standard Oil, and his wife Emily bonded over a shared love of Shakespeare. In 1889 Henry purchased his first rare book, and together he and Emily spent decades amassing the world's largest Shakespeare collection. In 1919 they bought a plot of land in Washington, DC to house the collection, and by the time it opened in 1932, they had accumulated over 200,000 items to fill it with.

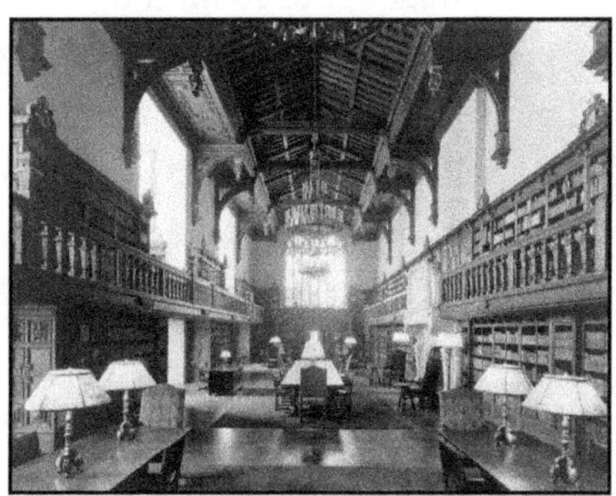

Today the library has expanded to include teaching and live performances. Long and short term fellowships are awarded through two annual competitions. Just as Shakespeare had his own sponsors, Folger Library fellowships are supported through generous sponsors like The National Endowment for the Humanities, The Andrew W. Mellon Foundation, and The American Council of Learned Societies.

After World War II, high tax rates on the wealthy would spur growth in the creation of trusts and foundations as tax shelters. Changes in the tax code allowed corporations to deduct charitable contributions up to 5 percent of taxable income. Now most major corporations have a corporate foundation, and charitable obligations to society have become an expected part of doing business.

Corporate foundations are private and tax-exempt. They start with a grant from the parent company and are funded with money from their pre-tax profit. The company's CEO and other executives sit on the board of directors and are responsible for a lot of the decision making as to where the foundation money is spent. Those executive officers can also serve on other community boards or private foundations. A community foundation is a regional foundation that is funded by many separate donors for the long-term benefit of those residents. Those funds are primarily permanent and their mission is broadly defined. They are supported by private and public donors from within the community and act as a grant-making foundation.

One trend that has sprung out of community foundations is called giving circles, where people pool their money, time, talent, and resources for the greater good of the community. Each member of the group participates in the decision-making process about which charitable entity will be funded and can include a wide range of causes. The majority of giving circles have typically been comprised of women, but now giving circles include all age groups and genders.

They can be started by members of the community who then go in search of a host organization. The benefits include increased diversity for the host donors, increased community involvement, and more opportunities for the existing host donors to learn more about what the actual needs of the community are and how they can support that community with grants. A co-created giving circle is a good way to combine the energy of the giving circle with the established business support of the host organization. The co-created giving circle should have a good balance of paid staff and volunteers. Another example is a giving circle that is started by the host organization itself that is established to meet specific needs in the community or to enhance services that can be offered to donors.

People will join a giving circle because they want to participate on a local level and be a part of something that will improve their community. This way they get to see firsthand where their donations are going. Giving circles appeal to people who have either never been philanthropists or who may not feel comfortable going the traditional route. These are usually people who have donated their time and money to the community on a different level.

Family foundations are foundations whose funds come from members of a single family. According to The Council on Foundations, at least one family member must serve as a board member or officer and as a donor. Most of those family members serve as trustees or directors on a voluntary basis. They represent more than half of all independent foundations. According to 2010 data from the Foundation Center, larger family foundations were more likely to donate to education and health than the arts. Family foundations are usually set up as a charitable trust. That money is invested and the revenue from it is used to give out grants. This is why a good strong economy is vital. A sluggish economy means less money for artists.

Getting a grant is similar to getting sponsorship since they both free you up to spend time on your craft as an artist without having to worry about paying the bills. And technically neither one of them has to be repaid, unlike a loan. But neither one is totally free money without any strings attached. You still have to live up to your responsibilities as an artist and deliver what you promise. Grants vary in their amounts, guidelines, and application process.

Sponsorship is a business agreement between two parties. The organization is looking to either increase sales or expand their profile in the community in a way that generates positive feelings for future, potential customers. Grants are not about increasing profits but still could be a way of a company expanding their profile in the community to generate good will, as it helps someone or a group of people in need.

The great news for artists is that there are many individuals and organizations that want to support artists. The trick is finding them, networking with them, and constantly getting your proposals in front of them. In David Callahan's book *The Givers: Wealth, Power, and Philanthropy in a New Gilded Age*, he shines a light on the new generation of top mega philanthropists and how they're using their philanthropy for power and influence: "From 2003 to 2013, according to one study, itemized charitable contributions from people making $500,000 or more increased by 57%, while itemized contributions from people making $10,000,000 or more increased by 104% over the same period."[24]

---

24 David Callahan, *The Givers: Wealth, Power, and Philanthropy in a New Gilded*

Not all of them are giving their money to art, but there are plenty who are. Like Michael Bloomberg, whose Arts Innovation and Management group has committed over $64 million to provide support to arts and cultural organizations in New York City. This money supplies grants to around 250 small and medium sized dance, film, literature, theater, music, and visual arts organizations. In 2015 he created the Public Arts Challenge to provide support to temporary public art projects as a way of revitalizing cities. It does this by calling on other mayors to work with the artists to develop those public art projects that may benefit their cities, either visually or through increased tourism.

Another philanthropist who believes in local and regional arts funding is cable TV billionaire Amos Hostetter, Jr. and his wife Barbara. Their Barr Foundation focuses their philanthropy on their home state of Massachusetts, and primarily in Boston, where they are located. They are one of the largest private foundations in New England. According to their mission statement:

"Our mission is to invest in human, natural, and creative potential, serving as thoughtful stewards and catalysts." They believe that "Arts and creativity are essential for vibrant, vital, and engaged communities." Some of their grantees include mid-sized arts organizations such as Actors' Shakespeare Project, American Repertory Theater, Boston Ballet, Boston Center for the Arts, Boston Lyric Opera, Handel and Haydn Society, Institute of Contemporary Art, and Lyric Stage Company.

Another foundation that supports local and regional artists in the Denver, Colorado, area is the Bonfils-Stanton Foundation. As they note on their website, they support the arts because: "we believe that all people need and deserve the beauty, joy, and connections that the arts provide and inspire. When we support the arts, we foster personal growth and inspiration; we create more vibrant neighborhoods, overcome societal challenges in unique ways, our children become more well-rounded and successful, and our economy expands exponentially."

Age, Alfred A. Knopf, 2017, 18.

They continue: "Arts promote true prosperity. The arts are fundamental to our humanity. They ennoble and inspire us – fostering creativity, goodness, and beauty. The arts help us express our values, build bridges between cultures, and bring us together regardless of ethnicity, religion, or age. When times are tough, art is salve for the ache." Some of their grantees include Allied Arts, Americas for Conservation and the Arts, Art Students League of Denver, Augustana Arts, Central City Opera House, Children's Museum of Denver, and the Buntport Theatre Company.

The Fred A. and Barbara M. Erb Family Foundation is focused on the arts in the Detroit area, in the geographic areas of Wayne, Oakland, and Macomb counties in Michigan though they generally don't give out grants to individual artists. The Zellerbach Family Foundation focuses their attention on artists in the San Francisco Bay area, where the family has been active locally since 1868. The actual foundation was established in 1956 by Mrs. Jennie B. Zellerbach. They support both individuals and small to mid-size arts organizations. The ZFF has a long history of supporting the arts in the Bay Area, and its Community Arts program has awarded over $15 million in grants.

In her book "*Guide to Getting Arts Grants*", Ellen Liberatori lists some of the many grants available to artists:

- Organizational grants for arts programs
- Special projects
- Art career fellowships
- Short term fellowships
- Travel and study
- Mentoring grants
- Emerging artists grants
- Distinguished artists grants
- Arts collaboration grants
- Production grants to finish a work
- Peer learning grants for artists who work in nonprofits

According to the National Center for Charitable Statistics, there are over 1.5 million non-profits registered in the U.S. Most artist grants are given to artists who are in their mid-career phase. They have a body of work behind them that they can show as proof of their commitment. Usually an emerging artist is young, but that isn't always the case. Grandma Moses was an emerging artist at the age of 78. Laura Ingalls Wilder of *Little House on the Prairie* fame didn't even start writing until she was 44 and didn't start to make a name for herself until she was 64.

An emerging artist is simply one who is in the early stage of their career. They've made the decision to make art their lifelong career and are just learning the ropes within their chosen field.

A mid-career artist has a body of work to show and has achieved a certain level of notoriety over several years. By then you should have a list of reputable people in the industry who can vouch for you, and some press to back that up. An established artist has achieved a certain level of fame and has an extensive body of work to show for it. Many artists stay in mid-career for quite a while before moving up to established artist.

Former art gallerist Carlos Rivera has elevated the mystique of the emerging artist by using data-driven speculation to create the highly successful and wildly disruptive website Art Rank. Data mining and algorithms alert subscribers about the perfect time to buy or sell an emerging artist's work. It treats art more as a commodity than something you would buy because you're passionate about it. Some critics are against the idea of judging the work of an emerging artist before their careers have had a chance to develop.

Private foundations step in and provide grants where they are needed, like when the Dorothea and Leo Rabkin Foundation announced an annual prize of $50,000 to American art writers who write for general audiences, since major publications have been cutting down on their art coverage. As ad revenue has fallen tremendously, theater and arts reviews have been cut from newspapers like the *New*

York Times. Many freelancers were put out of work, not just at the *Times* but at newspapers around the country. The Dorothea and Leo Rabkin Foundation is giving some of those art critics a second chance.

When museums around the country were reeling from the global recession, private foundations stepped in to help. But philanthropists these days are asking for more measurable results from their generous donations. They want their money to make the biggest impact possible, like being able to have free admission to the museums, which has increased museum attendance. Much philanthropy is also now being done more on a local level. The money invested in a local or regional museum goes further.

One of the most well-known foundations is the MacArthur Foundation. The MacArthur Fellows awards (which have come to be known as the "genius" grants) provide "unrestricted fellowships to talented individuals who have shown extraordinary originality and dedication in their creative pursuits and a marked capacity for self-direction," according to their website. Fellows are selected according to the following criteria: exceptional creativity, future promise based on past accomplishments, and the potential for the fellowship to spawn even more creative work.

The MacArthur awards fellowships directly to individuals, such as writers, scientists, artists, social scientists, humanists, teachers, and entrepreneurs, rather than through institutions. Recipients can use the grant however they wish, even to change fields or career if they wish. It is an investment in a person's potential and does not require any reports or evaluations—it is a "no strings attached" award of $625,000 paid out over 5 years. An independent selection committee selects 20-30 fellows each year who are reflective of America's diversity. The committee doesn't accept unsolicited nominations or applications.

Crowdfunding and Other Financing

*"Get the confidence of the public and you will have
no difficulty in getting their patronage."*

Harry Gordon Selfridge

Before crowdfunding if you wanted to raise money for your art project you could either ask friends and family for a loan, ask the bank for a loan, or get angel investors to buy into your company. Just like sponsorship, crowdfunding, or getting funding from multiple people to finance a new business venture, has been around since the 1700s. But it has recently seen a resurgence in the past couple of decades with the popularity of the internet.

It's been my experience working with creative people that most are more right brained than left brained. And the entrepreneurial artist has to have some level of business sense if they want to create their own destiny. But it is a skill that can be learned. Crowdfunding is a form of patronage. The difference is that the investment comes from a large number of patrons who are passionate about a particular artist or project. And the artist or project must build communities of these passionate people who are willing to open their checkbooks to their crowdfunding campaign.

There's never been a better time to be an artist because of all of the different ways to get around the traditional gatekeepers. But to be successful you have to take on the duties that the gatekeeper would have taken care of, like buying rights to properties or writing your own, promoting a project and distribution, which is the business side. I learned a lot about the business side of the film and TV business when I moved from being in front of the camera to working behind the camera

Years ago I worked as a film and TV distributor in Hollywood. Part of my job was buying the rights to films and TV shows. I attended all of the film and TV markets like Cannes, MIPCOM, MIPTV, American Film Market, etc. I went from being an actor and begging for a job to being a top-level gatekeeper who bought the rights to those same projects. As a distributor, those same people who turned me down for acting jobs were suddenly begging me to buy their films and TV shows. It was an enviable position to be in.

I received invitations to the best parties in town and was treated to the finest restaurants. Anyone could make a movie, but you still had to get it distributed. Every weekend I would spend hours going through viewing copies sent to me in the hopes of finding a handful of gems we wanted to distribute. Most of them were lower budget, independent films and TV shows.

Every area of the entertainment industry has always been controlled by a gatekeeper who held on to their power by limiting access to resources artists needed, such as distribution. The old Hollywood studio system is a good example. Stars were under-contract employees of the studio. Those contracts had morality clauses to protect the images their studios had created for them. Actors didn't have the right to choose which movies they wanted to star in, and they would be suspended if they declined to do a certain movie.

A small handful of studios controlled the entire film process from start to finish and kept actors, writers and directors under strict contracts. It was a system closed to anyone who wasn't able to get through the gate. The studios even controlled the theaters where the movies were shown until they were challenged under anti-trust laws and forced to separate production from distribution and exhibition. Another anti-trust lawsuit involved block booking, a system of selling multiple films to a theater as one unit. The Hollywood studio system ended by the 1960s when studios could no longer afford to keep dozens of writers, actors and directors under contract.

Suddenly a new system was born that utilized agents and casting directors. Star actors, directors, and writers were still in demand, but now about half of all films were made by independent producers. By 1957, the overseas market grew to become 40-50 percent of Hollywood's total revenue, and stars were now asking for a percentage of profits instead of a salary. Independent producers were making half of all movies made in America.

Some actors, writers and directors began to see the benefit of becoming their own entrepreneurial gatekeepers. Stars like Frank Sinatra and Gregory Peck were buying scripts and creating their own production companies. Charlie Chaplin, Mary Pickford, Douglas Fairbanks and D.W. Griffith had been their own gatekeepers since they collectively formed United Artists in 1919. They all wanted to have more creative and financial control over their careers. Today, stars like Adam Sandler, Leonardo DiCaprio, Queen Latifah, Will Smith, Drew Barrymore, and Tom Cruise, all have their own production companies.

Actor Billy Bob Thornton knew the best path to stardom was to create that path himself. While looking for acting work in Hollywood, he was also writing on the side. His first break happened after co-writing and staring in the 1992 thriller *One False Move*. But it was his performance of slow-witted Carl in the independent film *Sling Blade*, that he also wrote and directed, that catapulted him into international fame and won him an Academy award for best adapted screenplay.

Friends Ben Affleck and Matt Damon turned their careers around with the production of *Good Will Hunting*, a film that they co-wrote and Damon starred in. The idea for the script was born while Damon was in college at Harvard. It started out as a forty-page script written as an assignment for a drama class. It would take years to actually see the film made, but it turned out to be a star project for both of them, winning nine Academy Awards.

But, it's not just celebrities who create and produce their own material. Clever up and coming actors, writers, and directors are now becoming double and triple threats. Once seen as being cheesy to be a hyphenate, it's now one of the best ways to push past the gatekeepers and write, direct, and star in your own productions. Actress Brit Marling came to Hollywood and found it much the same as other actors. Being an unknown and breaking into Hollywood is daunting. The roles for someone in that position are basically "girl #1" or bit parts with nudity. Brit realized if she wanted to get better parts, she would have to write them herself. So that's what she did. She wrote, produced, and starred in the films *Another Earth* and *Sound of My Voice*, which debuted at Sundance to critical acclaim.

Now there are many different ways to get projects such as these funded. We mentioned crowdfunding earlier, and there are over 1,000 crowdfunding platforms to choose from, including my own called Indie Sponsor. Indie Sponsor is also an online directory for artists seeking small business sponsorship. I've worked as a publicist on several crowdfunding campaigns, and I believe that even more important than publicity is having a big network in place before you even think about starting a crowdfunding campaign.

Crowdfunding is about building a community around a project and getting backers excited and interested enough to open their wallets and give you money to see that it happens.

Having that initial financial support is critical. Nobody wants to be the first to donate money. It may take having you, your parents, and your friends jumpstart it by putting in some money. Once people see that others are willing to support you they will often jump on the bandwagon. If you at least put in 5 percent you have a 50 percent chance of reaching your goal, as opposed to only 15 percent for those crowdfunding campaigns that start off with no money. Aim to raise 15 percent in the beginning through yourself, family, and friends, and about 20 percent through your face to face launch party.

Having a reasonable and reachable goal, and making a detailed breakdown of expenses, is also important. You don't want to ask for too much or people will think "why bother." Ask for just enough so that you can get the project off the ground. Don't forget to include the following expenses in your spreadsheet:

- Marketing expenses
- Publicity
- Administrative
- Shipping
- Insurance
- Rewards

The pre-launch stage is the most important part of a crowdfunding campaign. With each of the campaigns I worked on, the ones that were most successful allowed at least three months for the pre-launch phase. This is assuming you already have a large, solid network. If you don't, you need to allow much more time to build one up. This includes backing other people's projects. If you want to really be successful as a crowdfunder, you need to spend some time on the other side. What projects catch your attention? Study their campaigns and videos. What makes you laugh or touches your heart? Philanthropic projects are all about emotion. Make sure your video touches people in some way by either making them laugh, cry, or think.

You also need to make sure you have a blog up and running before you start. Blogs don't get picked up by Google overnight, so if you don't have one at all, wait until your blog is a little more popular before you start your campaign. You want to keep people in the loop during the whole process, and the best way is by sending them emails and posting your info on your blog.

Reach out to other bloggers who write about your topic and read their blogs. Post interesting and helpful information on their blogs before reaching out to see if you could write a post for them. Not all bloggers will do that, but if you can, you expand your network quickly with people who are already into your topic. This helps establish yourself as an expert.

Joseph Hogue, author of *Step by Step Crowdfunding: Everything You Need to Raise Money From the Crowd*, suggests interviewing an expert for your blog who has a strong social media following by searching for recently published books on similar subjects through Amazon. He also suggests finding service providers in your crowdfunding campaign's area and asking other bloggers if they'd be interested in being interviewed for your blog or podcast.

Spend time hanging out in forums where there are people who would be passionate and interested in your project. Make friends. Answer questions. Be helpful. Those same people will remember you and will be willing to help return the favor when you're ready for your launch. Even if they don't donate money, they will probably be willing to send your campaign info out through their social media and tell others about it. Any help you can get is valuable, including volunteers for launch parties.

A launch party is one of the best things you can do if you plan to be a successful crowdfunder. I have a friend who raised $5,000 in one night by doing a launch party. He makes it a point to make friends everywhere he goes. He does so many favors for other people that when he decided to have a launch party for his crowdfunding campaign the place was sold out. Friends brought their friends and everyone passed the word around. Someone contacted the media, who interviewed my friend for a lengthy article in a local newspaper.

In the digital age, where sending emails is the easy way out, nothing beats face to face for success in business. Yes, it's old school, but it works! A launch party doesn't have to be fancy, and it shouldn't be expensive. Backers want to know their money is being spent wisely. But that doesn't mean you shouldn't be creative.

Klaudia Kovacs is a multi-award-winning Hollywood film & theater director who regularly crowdfunds her own projects. She is also known as "The Crowdfunding Queen" as she teaches others how to crowdfund their own projects effectively. Klaudia is regularly invited as a public speaker to share her secrets of successful crowdfunding and has spoken at several Ivy League universities, the American Film Institute (AFI), AFTRA-SAG, and many international film festivals. Here's what she had to say in a recent interview:

As a director, I waited for a decade for someone to give me an opportunity in show business but that only happens in the movies... So, I crowdfunded my first film and raised 1.7 million dollars.

The most important part about a successful launch party is to create a solid (read: interested) crowd first. Take as much time as you can to find your crowd, cultivate a strong relationship with them, and involve them emotionally before starting your campaign. Especially, if you're raising a lot of money, it's crucial that your crowd trusts you with large sums. Building trust doesn't happen overnight so that needs to be part of your plan.

Before my launch party and during my crowdfunding process, I followed the Rule of Seven which is a marketing adage. It says that a prospect needs to see/hear/read your marketing message at least seven times before they take action. I mixed up the forms of communication (phone calls, emails, newsletters, videos, social media, personal meetings, etc.) with my crowd and made sure that it wasn't too often for them to feel crowded but often enough that they would not forget about my film.

I also did a lot of research and tried to make an educated guess about which individuals would be my high-end donors, and focused my attention on them. It's not the quantity of donors but the quality of the launch party that will make you successful.

I had multiple launch parties nationally and internationally and I always tried to attend in person which helped a lot. To keep the premiere status of the launch parties alive, I named the events after each location, such as Los Angeles Launch Party, Seattle Launch Party, Toronto Launch Party, etc. This way I was able to have endless launch parties and still make the local crowd feel like number one.

By the way, always treat everyone like a VIP and you might end up with a miracle! There was a person who didn't give me a single dime but encouraged an investor to support my project with $150,000.

Last but not least, become a thank-you-machine BEFORE your launch party. Nothing will inspire people more than you displaying professionalism, commitment, grace, and gratitude. The more you acknowledge people the more they will support you. Don't ever feel odd about thanking someone multiple times. Being grateful is not something you can ever overdo.[25]

Even celebrities who are already established are using crowdfunding to finance new projects. A well-known example is Zack Braff, of *Scrubs* fame, who went on Kickstarter to raise $2 million for his film *Wish I Was Here*. He reached his goal and more in only 48 hours and got a big backlash for it. Critics wondered why Braff had to ask the public for money for a film they wouldn't make a profit on. Yet over 47,000 people donated to the campaign, which included perks such as T-shirts and an advanced online screening.

Braff, like other entrepreneurs who have tried crowdfunding, had to work the creative side and the business side. With crowdfunding you also have to deal with the perks, such as T-shirts, which also adds an extra layer of work. That's part of the deal when you ask for money from the public. He said that he mostly did it this way to enable him to maintain creative control over the way the film turned out. Going the traditional route means giving up your right to location casting choices and budget considerations. In other words, "the final cut" in how your film will be shot and edited. But even though he raised $3.1 million and got the film he wanted, he said he wouldn't be using the crowdfunding method again.

In my days of working as a distributor and financier I can tell you that we demanded these things too when we were the ones putting up the money. It's simple. He who has the gold rules. We also had a pre-approved list of actors that would "play" in Europe and other parts of the world. No matter how popular the actor was in the U.S., if we couldn't sell the film rights in Spain or Germany, it didn't matter.

---

25 http://klaudiakovacs.com/publicspeakingandconsulting/

Films aren't the only things being crowdfunded, and it isn't the only place to find celebrities. Freddie Wong became a You Tube star after winning the Guitar Hero 2 competition at the World Series of Video Games in Dallas, Texas, in 2007. He now has over 4 million You Tube subscribers and has dipped his toe into crowdfunding for his web TV series "Video Game High School." His media company RocketJump raised $808 thousand from 10,613 backers in February 2013 for the show's second series.

Writers are also getting in on the crowdfunding act like Charles Dickens did years ago when he sold advertising space in his books. Writers use crowdfunding to guarantee a certain amount of money upfront before they start writing the book. They get the benefits of having an advance without being at the mercy of a publisher.

Or if you are interested in having a traditional publisher and still want to crowdfund your book, check out Publishizer, a crowdfunding platform for authors. The way Publishizer works is that you first write and submit a professional proposal. Then a thirty-day campaign is launched and pre-orders for the book are taken. Top performing proposals go out to readers every week. Then at the end of the campaign, publishers get the list and they decide if they want to take on the book. Publishizer doesn't get in the middle of negotiations, but does take 30 percent of the crowdfunded amount raised, and you receive the rest. Then you negotiate your own deal with the publisher.

In the past, a writer, for example, would work with a publisher and get an advance. Then the publisher would handle all of the designing, printing, selling and promotion. As an entrepreneurial writer who wants to self-publish you have to do all of that yourself, including coming up with the money. But with crowdfunding you can at least raise the money to do it, and creative control is all in your hands.

Hybrid authors earn more money than traditionally published authors and self-published authors, according to a survey conducted by Digital Book World. This is a new, up and coming strategy for authors that is proving to be successful. But, whether you plan to self-publish, sign with a traditional publisher, or become a hybrid author, you still need to start building your network. Many publishers want you to have a list of over 100,000 people before they will take you seriously. Seth Godin raised $287,342 for his book *The Icarus Deception* through crowdfunding. He also has a huge following of fans who will read anything he writes.

If you want to self-publish, it's even more important to have a following. And if you're going to do it through crowdfunding, it's vital. No matter how your book is published, you must be ready to either promote it yourself or help someone else promote it. Books don't sell themselves. I've handled PR for celebrities with books, and their publishers expect them to get out and hustle just like they do.

Performing artist Marina Abramovic is known for her controversial and dangerous performances pieces, which have tested her limits physically, mentally and emotionally. Her art is a collaborative give and take with the audience, and she is still challenging herself as a performing artist in her 70s, long after many in the profession would have retired.

In Edinburgh in 1973, she made use of twenty knives and two tape recorders as she played the Russian game where rhythmic knife jabs are aimed between the player's splayed-out fingers. When she cut herself Abramovic picked up another knife, recording herself the whole time. Then she replayed the tape, listening carefully, and replicated her actions thus merging the present with the past. Another one of her first pieces, "I am the object", where the audience was encouraged to do whatever they wanted to her body with a choice of 72 objects. The objects were things as innocuous as a feather, rose, honey and Band-Aids to more violent ones such as a gun, bullets, whip, scissors, and a saw. Half of the audience sought to protect her, while half of the audience became more and more violent.

She developed such a following, or some would say a cult, that when she recently decided to crowdfund, her followers responded enthusiastically. Her life's body of work speaks for itself, but she had an epiphany while working on a piece for the New York Museum of Modern Art where she invited the audience to spend time in a chair across from her just gazing into her eyes. She realized how important her work with audience participation was and wanted to preserve it in a permanent way. She started a Kickstarter campaign for the Marina Abramovic Institute, which would blend science, technology, and spirituality in long durational work that involved the audience in the work. Her funding goal was $600,000 and she surpassed that with 4,765 backers contributing $661,452.

Another performing artist who found success crowdfunding is Tim Lacatena. Lacatena was a working actor in Los Angeles who went on over 1300 auditions in a span of thirteen years. But creatively he felt something was missing. He longed for the days of artistic immersion he had when he was younger and training in a ballet studio eight hours a day. A chance improv class led to an epiphany and the creation of a digital sketch collaborative called Nightpantz. Lacatena started wrangling the best talent he could find, from actors, directors, producers, sound mixers, cinematographers, editors and composers. He found a brilliant and hard-working group of artists who wanted to create their own destinies without having to wait for projects to find them.

The Nightpantz crew steadily grew their collaborative to include anyone who was talented and willing to work hard. What also grew over time was their fan base. So when they finally decided to do their first Kickstarter campaign, they already had a solid following. Also, having over 200 members who all acted as a promotional arm for the group didn't hurt. Their Kickstarter campaign goal was $10,000 for their second season and would go to make at least 25 new sketches. They raised almost $13,000. The group now has their own mascot, Walter the Catfish, and a slogan, "Relax and

Get (Un) Comfortable," which you'll find on their own limited edition T-shirts.

Nightpantz is a great example of simply starting with whatever you have, even if it's no money or connections. Sponsors want to see that you've at least done something to get started, and the more you have in your portfolio, the better. Prove to them that you're here to stay and that you have a solid base behind you. Start putting out good work and building a fan base. Sponsors will supply the funding, but you supply the talent, innovation, and hard work. Prove that you run your career like a business that will bring them a good ROI.

Tom Siddell started out writing and drawing his comics as a hobby, but now thanks to his many patrons on Patreon, he is able to focus on it full-time. Patreon is an innovative way for artists to connect with their fans, who support them on a monthly basis, so they can continue to create the kind of work those fans enjoy. Another Patreon artist, Julien Neel, is a one man barbershop quartet who has been putting together videos of Beatles songs and old classics. It isn't the only way he makes money as an artist, but it's just one stream of reliable revenue.

Patreon was started by Jack Conte who was trying to figure out how to capitalize on his popular You Tube videos. He partnered with Sam Yam to create a membership style website that allows artists to accept donations on a monthly basis for works in progress. Patreon raised over $47 million from investors who receive exclusive behind the scenes content and experiences from their favorite artists. So, artists get to do what they do best… create. And Patreon handles all of the business responsibilities, while only taking a 5 percent commission. Some of the artists on Patreon include writers, musicians, dancers, podcasters, painters, animators, illustrators, and photographers.

Musicians are also turning to crowdfunding and bypassing the gatekeeper. The music industry, like every other creative industry, has always worked on the gatekeeper system. A talented musician would have to hold their hand out and beg to be seen or heard by a "suit" at a record label who had the power to say yes or no and potentially crush the dreams of an artist they didn't want to represent. Times have changed, and an entrepreneurial artist now has the power given back to them if they really want to put the work into doing it themselves and taking control of their music's distribution and promotion, thanks to the internet and social media. One artist who has been quite successful without a record label is Amanda Palmer and her band The Grand Theft Orchestra. Their new album was completely funded by Kickstarter to the tune of (no pun intended) $1,192,793. This is the highest funded music project so far on Kickstarter.

The old system where artists received earnings from an album release were based on physical costs. Digital distribution and streaming services like Spotify, Pandora, Apple Music, Google Play, and iTunes, make it easier to get paid for their music. And there are plenty of ways for artists to go straight to the end user... their fans. Create your own sound early on and let your fans grow with you. They not only want to hear your music, but they also want to hear your story and be a part of your community. They want to see the behind the scenes experience, so videotape your practice sessions and show the process.

Create a Facebook artist page and start getting fans that way. Keep your personal and professional Facebook pages separate. Post just enough but not too much. Make sure you build up credibility and trust first. Promote your gigs locally with social media and a little bit of local advertising. Boost it on Facebook and Twitter, post pictures and videos of previous shows, and a teaser of a show to come. Don't overlook public relations. I handled the PR for an actor who had played significant roles in movies and TV shows who had never even considered doing any PR. I instantly got him on two local TV stations when his last film came out.

TV and radio shows, magazines, and bloggers are always looking for great guests who have new books, albums, and live events going on. Put together press pictures, bios, tour dates, etc. and start getting the word out to the public. Network with everyone you know without making yourself a pest. A good way to promote yourself is to give away free T-shirts and hats with your band's name on them. You can give them away at your live events or online in exchange for a picture of fans wearing the shirts or hats. You can also sell them at your live concerts. Either way, it's a great way to advertise your band.

Get fans to sign up for your newsletter online while at the show. Sell them a recording of what they just heard in concert. There's never a better time to get them interested than when they are live at your event and a captive audience member. They're already excited about you. Make sure you lock them in to hear about future events, music, and behind the scenes exclusives.

Just like actors usually think they have to have an agent or a manager, musicians also tend to believe the same thing. No agent or manager wants to take 10-20 percent of nothing when you are just starting out. Spend your time and money building your career yourself and those people will eventually find you, believe me. By then you might not even need them.

I'm sure I've said it a million times in this book, but if you're going to be an entrepreneurial artist you have to hustle to promote yourself. Anyone can create a piece of art, but without promotion it's like a sign in the desert. If you want to make money as an artist, just get used to it and learn to like it. If you want to take the entrepreneurial route in your career it helps to learn how to raise money. Unlike crowdfunding or grants, which don't have to be paid back, angel investors, sponsors, or venture capitalists want a return on their money. They want proof that the projects they fund will be a good return on investment.

Before you start looking for investors, Morrie Warshawski has some great advice in his book *Shaking the Money Tree: The Art of Getting Grants and Donations for Film and Video Projects*. The book is primarily for filmmakers, but most of the advice is relevant to other artists as well.

He has clients create a mission statement telling why they are making this project and what they hope to accomplish by doing it. As he says, "The most important aspect of the mission statement is its ability to help the filmmaker articulate and commit to a unique sense of purpose that keeps her centered, and broadcasts to all potential funders and clients that this is a person who is serious about her work, and knows what she wants to accomplish. No one wants to work with or fund a filmmaker who is unclear about this central issue."[26]

Always put yourself in the shoes of the funder or patron and look at it from a financial viewpoint instead of just from the creative side. Is your project a good investment? Or is it a passion project that would do better with crowdfunding or grants? People will give their money to something they feel passionate about as a crowdfunder or grantor, but if they are looking for a return on it, it needs to have more to it than that. By the way, there's no rule that says you can't do a combination of crowdfunding, venture capital, angel investors, grants, or sponsorship. If you plan on staying in the nonprofit arena, you can either start you own 501(c) 3 or you can look for a fiscal sponsor who already has a nonprofit set up.

According to the National Network of Fiscal Sponsors website: "Fiscal sponsorship generally entails a nonprofit organization (the "fiscal sponsor") agreeing to provide administrative services and oversight to, and assume some or all of the legal and financial responsibility for, the activities of groups or individuals engaged in work that relates to the fiscal sponsor's mission.

---

26 Morrie Warshawski, *Shaking the Money Tree: The Art of Getting Grants and Donations for Film and Video*, Michael Weise Productions, 2010, 2.

Fiscal sponsors are tax-exempt, charitable ventures that, according to a recent IRS report "have the ability to receive charitable contributions for specific projects, the infrastructure to ensure compliance with applicable federal and state laws and adequate internal controls to ensure that the funds will be used for the intended charitable purposes."[27]

A popular fiscal sponsor among artists is Fractured Atlas, founded by CEO Adam Huttler. The organization is legally registered to fundraise in all fifty states. There is a 7 percent administrative fee on all donations. This allows you to fundraise without having to set up your own nonprofit, which can be costly and time consuming. This leaves you more time to focus on creating. Fractured Atlas's business model is based on a mix of earned and contributed revenue that helps ensure that it remains a community-oriented resilient organization.

A good place to start with all these funding sources is a vision statement: Where do you see yourself as an artist several years from now? What do you intend to accomplish in those years? Put some time into this, and it will allow you to be more strategic and see the bigger picture.

---

27 http://www.fiscalsponsors.org/pages/about-fiscal-sponsorship

The Future of the Arts

"The Best Way to Predict Your Future is to Create It"

Abraham Lincoln

No one has a crystal ball to accurately predict the future, but if you want to know the future, you must know the past, and watch where things are trending. There's never been a better time to be an artist, whether you're a literary, performing, or fine artist. The gatekeepers of the past are slowly losing their power, and technology is turning artists of all kinds into entrepreneurs.

New art is being created, along with new art forms, and artists are pushing the boundaries on their own terms, like Geoffrey Drake Brockman, a cybernetic artist who has combined his background as a computer programmer and his skills as an artist to make art that is interactive with an audience. Fire artists are able to "paint" images in the air using pixels instead of real fire. The performance is animated first and then coordinated with a live artist who paints images, graphics, text, and logos in the air.

The way we consume media is also changing. Henry Jenkins explains what media converge is in *Convergence Culture: Where Old and New Media Collide*: "the flow of content across multiple media platforms, the cooperation between multiple media industries, and the migratory behavior of media audiences who will go almost anywhere in search of the kinds of entertainment experiences they want." The delivery technologies that we use to view media always change, while media is always evolving.[28] Futurists imagine music as being more immersive, including full body suits with microscopic sensors so you can also feel the music through vibrations.

Storytelling has evolved from tales told around the campfire. Transmedia storytelling or "multi-platform" storytelling is becoming more popular. Thanks to technology, we can tell stories from different viewpoints and using different platforms. *Uneasy Lies the Mind* hails itself as the first feature-length narrative to be shot entirely on an iPhone. Director Ricky Fosheim raised $10,000 from a crowdfunding campaign to get the movie made.

Netflix began as a subscription service where you rent movies for a monthly rate on an unlimited basis. You couldn't get a new movie until you returned the one you had—therefore no late fees. In 2007 they started streaming movies. And several years later they were producing their own original programming. "House of Cards" became a hit and was the first online-only web show to earn an Emmy nomination.

Thanks to the internet, anyone can now become the star of their own show without having to get the approval of a gatekeeper like a museum curator, art critic, gallery owner, book publisher, theatrical agent, casting director or producer. In the past, fine art was only for the wealthy, created by them and owned by them, while the masses were simply allowed to view them. Now art is for everyone. Created by everyone, owned by everyone, and now thanks to crowdfunding, grants and sponsorship... funded by everyone.

So, where do you see yourself as an artist several years from now? Will you still be holding your hand out begging someone

---

28 Henry Jenkins, *Convergence Culture: Where Old and New Media Collide*, New York University Press, 2006, 13.

to give you a job? Or will you be creating your own career using patronage? I can't wait to see what the next generation of Leonardo di Vincis will create!

INDIE SPONSOR

Never before in history have we had so many small and large businesses who could be potential sponsors for artists of all kinds. At Indie Sponsor we intend to bridge the gap between art and business. Our goal is to put an end to the starving artist mentality and teach artists how to run their careers like a business.

Most large corporations already know that it makes good sense to partner with artists, and have signed on to social responsibility in that area. But there are over 28 million small businesses who are hungry to play with the big boys and compete with their own sponsorship. That's where we come in. Indie Sponsor is the liaison between the artist and the sponsoring corporation or small business. We specialize in small business sponsorship and large corporate regional and local sponsorship.

At Indie Sponsor we're the liaison between the artist who creates a unique creative opportunity, and corporations, big and small, who would be happy to sponsor them and become their collaborators and financial partners.

Sponsorship is a multi-billion dollar industry that keeps growing every year, no matter what the economy looks like. We want artists to get their share of that rapidly growing pie and stand on their own as working artists.

The job of an artist is unlike any other profession. Quite often it's either feast or famine. But that isn't enough to stop the creative type, who simply must create to feed their soul. We just want you to feed yourselves at the same time.

Check it out at:

www.indiesponsor.com

BIBLIOGRAPHY

Alexander, Victoria D. *Museums and Money: The Impact of Funding on Exhibitions, Scholarship, and Management* (Bloomington, IN: Indiana University Press, 1996).

Balfe, Judith Huggins, ed. *Paying the Piper: Causes and Consequences of Art Patronage* (Springfield, IL: University of Illinois Press, 1993).

Barnouw, Erik. *The Sponsor: Notes on a Modern Potentate* (New York, NY: Transaction, 1978).

Bourdua, Louise. *The Franciscans and Art Patronage in Late Medieval Italy* (New York, NY: Cambridge University Press, 2011).

Chansky, Dorothy. *Composing Ourselves: The Little Theatre Movement and the American Audience* (Carbondale, IL: Southern Illinois University Press, 2004).

Codell, Julie F., ed. *The Political Economy of Art: Making the Nation of Culture* (Vancouver, BC: Fairleigh Dickinson University Press, 2008).

Cuno, James, ed. *Whose Muse? Art Museums and the Public Trust* (Princeton, NJ: Princeton University Press, 2006).

Diymusician – http://diymusician.cdbaby.com/music-rights/3-ways-to-earn-money-from-your-music-on-spotify/

Evans, Chad. *Frontier Theatre: A History of 19th Century Theatrical Entertainment in the Canadian Far West and Alaska* (Victoria, BC: Sono Nis Press, 1983).

Field, Alan L., Michael O' Hare, and J. Mark Schuster. *Patrons Despite Themselves: Taxpayers and Arts Policy* (New York, NY: New York University Press, 1983).

Finn, David and Judith A. Jedlicka. *The Art of Leadership: Building Business-Arts Alliances* (New York, NY: Abbeville Press, 1998).

Fletcher, Pamela and Anne Helmreich, eds. *The Rise of the Modern Art Market in London, 1850-1939* (Manchester, UK: Manchester University Press, 2013 reprint).

Foss, Michael. *The Age of Patronage: The Arts in Society, 1660-1750* (New York, NY: Hamilton, 1971).

Garber, Marjorie. *Patronizing the Arts* (Princeton, NJ: Princeton University Press, 2008).

Glixon, David M. *The Muse of Gold – Art Patronage Through the Ages* (Bloomington, IN: AuthorHouse, 2006).

Global Media Commission of the International Advertising Agency. *Sponsorship: It's Role and Effects* (New York, NY: International Advertising Agency, 1988).

Gold, Barbara, ed. *Literary and Artistic Patronage in Ancient Rome* (Austin, TX: University of Texas Press, 1982).

Goldstein, Barbara, ed. *Public Art by the Book* (Wash., D.C.: Americans for the Arts, 2005).

Goldthwaite, Richard A. *Wealth and the Demand for Art in Italy 1300-1600* (Baltimore, MD: Johns Hopkins University Press, 1993).

Grampp, William D. *Pricing the Priceless: Art, Artists and Economics* (New York, NY: Basic Books, 1989).

Grieve, Victoria. *Federal Art Project and the Creation of Middlebrow Culture* (Urbana-Champaign, IL: University of Illinois Press, 2009).

Haskell, Francis. *Patrons and Painters: A Study in the Relations Between Italian Art and Society in the Age of the Baroque* (New Haven, CT: Yale University Press, 1980).

Heins, Marjorie. *Sex, Sin, and Blasphemy: A Guide to America's Censorship Wars* (New York, NY: The New Press, 1993)

Hersey, George L. *High Renaissance Art in St. Peter's and the Vatican* (Chicago, IL: University of Chicago Press, 1993).

Hibbert, Christopher. *The House of Medici: Its Rise and Fall* (New York, NY: William Morrow Paperbacks, 1991).

Hillman, Howard and Karin Abarbanel. *The Art of Winning Foundation Grants* (Public Services Material Ctr, 1989).

Hogue, Joseph. *Step by Step Crowdfunding: Everything You Need to Raise Money From the Crowd* (Efficient Alpha, 2015).

Hollingsworth, Mary. *Art in World History* (London, UK: Routledge, 2003).

Homberger, Eric. *Mrs. Astor's New York: Money & Social Power in a Gilded Age* (New Haven, CT: Yale University Press, 2004).

Hook, Phillip. "What Makes Art Sell? 10 Questions That Establish the Value of a Painting." *Huffington Post*. 30 Sept. 2014. www.huffingtonpost.com/phillip-hook-/ten-questions-that-establ_b_5884762.html

Hurst, Samantha. "Crowdfunding at its Best: Top 12 Successfully Funded Kickstarter and Indie GoGo Films." 20 Sept. 2014. www.crowdfundinsider.com

Kaiden, Nina and Bartlett Hayes. *Artist and Advocate: An Essay on Corporate Patronage* (Wash. D.C.: Americans for the Arts, 1966).

Kaiser, Michael. "Corporate Support for the Arts: A Changing Landscape." Huffington Post. www.huffingtonpost.com/michael-kaiser/corporate-support-for-the_b853148.html

Kent, Dale. *Cosimo de' Medici and the Florentine Renaissance: The Patron's Oeuvre* (New Haven, CT: Yale University Press, 2000).

Kunhardt, Phillip Jr., Phillip Kunhardt III, and Peter Kunhardt. *P.T. Barnum: America's Greatest Showman* (New York, NY: Knopf, 1995).

Larson, Gary O. *Reluctant Patron: The United States Government and the Arts, 1943-1965* (Philadelphia, PA: University of Pennsylvania Press, 1983).

Lesser, Casey. "11 of the world's most unusual artist residencies." www.artsy.net/article/artsy-editorial-11-of-the-world-s-most-unusual-artist-residencies

Levy, Alan Howard. *Government and the Arts: Debates over Federal Support of the Arts in America from George Washington to Jesse Helms* (Lantham, MD: University Press of America, 1997)

Loebl, Suzanne. *America's Medicis: The Rockefellers and Their Astonishing Cultural Legacy* (New York, NY: Harper, 2010).

Macleod, Dianne Sachko. *Art and the Victorian Middle Class: Money and the Making of Cultural Identity* (New York, NY: Cambridge University Press, 1996).

Marrow, Deborah. *Art Patronage of Maria de' Medici* (Ann Arbor, MI: UMI Research Press, 1982).

Martorella, Rosanne. *Art and Business: An International Perspective on Sponsorship* (Santa Barbara, CA: Praeger, 1996).

McLean, Paul D. *The Art of the Network: Strategic Interaction and Patronage in Renaissance Florence* (Durham, NC: Duke University Press, 2007).

Miller, Frank. *Censored Hollywood: Sex, Sin and Violence on Screen* (New York, NY: Turner, 1994).

Musicbed – http://www.musicbed.com/ knowledge-base/4-types-of-music-royalties/109

O'Farrell, Brian. *Shakespeare's Patron: William Herbert, Third Earl of Pembroke, 1580-1636: Politics, Patronage and Power* (London, UK: Bloomsbury, 2011).

O' Malley, Michelle. *The Business of Art: Contracts and the Commissioning Process in Renaissance Italy* (New Haven, CT: Yale University Press, 2007).

Rectanus, Mark W. *Culture Incorporated: Museums, Artists, and Corporate Sponsorships* (Minneapolis, MN: University of Minnesota Press, 2002).

Rockefeller, David. "50th Anniversary of Culture and the Corporation," Speech given 18 Nov. 2016 for the Americans for the Arts. www.americansforthearts.org/ news-room/americans-for-the-arts-news/50th-anniversary-of-culture-and-the-corporation-a-speech-by-david-rocke-feller

Schanke, Robert, ed. *Angels in the American Theater: Patrons, Patronage and Philanthropy* (Carbondale, IL: Southern Illinois University Press, 2007).

Smulyan, Susan. *Selling Radio: The Commercialization of American Broadcasting 1920-1934* (Washington, DC: Smithsonian, 1996).

Unger, Miles J. *Magnifico: The Brilliant Life and Violent Times of Lorenzo De' Medici* (New York, NY: Simon & Schuster, 2008).

Zuidervaart, Lambert. *Art in Public: Politics, Economics, and a Democratic Culture* (Cambridge, UK: Cambridge University Press, 2011).